UNDERWATER
TOOLS

DONALD J. HACKMAN, P.E.

Battelle Memorial Institute
Columbus Laboratories

DON W. CAUDY, P.E.

Battelle Memorial Institute
Columbus Laboratories

 BATTELLE PRESS
Columbus, Ohio

Library of Congress Cataloging in Publication Data
Hackman, Donald J., 1936–
Underwater tools.
Bibliography: p.
Includes index.
1. Ocean engineering—Equipment and supplies.
2. Underwater welding and cutting.
3. Diving, Submarine—Equipment and supplies.
I. Caudy, Don W., 1945–   II. Title.
TC1650.C38   681'.76   81-4399
ISBN: 0-934570-08-5   AACR2

PREFACE

THIS book was written for managers, engineers, scientists, divers, technicians, and students interested in or involved in using, fabricating, or designing underwater work systems. It brings together design and background information directly related to underwater work systems from reports, journals, manufacturers' catalogs and, most important, previously unpublished information developed by the authors during the course of their underwater work system design efforts. Many of the tables, graphs, and photographs come directly from the authors' files. The emphasis in this book is on the pragmatic engineering application aspects of each subject treated. Development and treatment of the theoretical background have been left to more specialized books, journals, and reports, many of which have been referenced.

ACKNOWLEDGMENTS

WE wish to express our gratitude to all who helped with this book, including the manufacturers and suppliers who generously contributed technical information and photographs; the management of Battelle Memorial Institute, who made facilities and personnel available to assist in the final editing of our manuscript; and Charles Robinson, who provided valuable editorial assistance in the preparation of our manuscript.

We wish especially to acknowledge the U.S. Navy's Naval Sea Systems Command, the Naval Ocean Systems Center, and the Office of Naval Research for their continuing support in underwater tool research and design. Special thanks must go to Dale G. Uhler of the Office of the Director of Ocean Engineering, Naval Sea Systems Command, and to John F. Freund of the Office of Ship Systems and Technology, Naval Sea Systems Command, for their support and encouragement in the preparation of this book. Special thanks also must go to Robert L. Wernli of the Ocean Technology Department, Naval Ocean Systems Center, for both his encouragement and his helpful editorial suggestions during the writing of this book.

Donald J. Hackman

Don W. Caudy

CONTENTS

UNDERWATER TOOLS   29

UNDERWATER POWER SOURCES   75

UNDERWATER DESIGN CONSIDERATIONS   87

COMPONENT SELECTION   101

6 UNDERWATER WORK SYSTEMS OF THE FUTURE   141

REFERENCES   145

INDEX   149

INTRODUCTION

MAN'S dependence upon the world's oceans for food, transportation, natural resources, and security results in a need to perform many important underwater tasks, such as maintenance and repair of ships, fabrication of structures to prevent beach erosion, recovery or salvage of sunken objects, and construction, inspection, and maintenance of offshore structures and pipelines. Much of this underwater work has been handled in essentially the same manner using essentially the same types of equipment as similar work performed on land. As a result, most of the commercially available tools used underwater to date are tools originally designed for dry use with a few minor modifications, such as protective coatings of grease, epoxy paint, or chromium plate for corrosion resistance, or a special handle for manipulator use (Penzias and Goodman 1973).

Although many standard tools can be used underwater with only minor modifications, the underwater environment generally degrades the performance of both the operator and the tool. Even a simple task like driving a nail, for example, becomes significantly more difficult underwater because of such environmental influences as limited visibility, resistance of the water to rapid movements, attenuation of the hammer blow at impact

1

due to water viscosity, restrictions caused by diving equipment and confined working spaces, and uncontrolled movement of the work piece or the diver. It is the job of the designer to provide tools that help the operator, whether it be a diver or a remote-controlled manipulator, overcome the limitations of the underwater environment.

For the most part, designers have handled this design task to date in more of an evolutionary than a revolutionary manner. For example, when a need arose to change tool bits underwater, designers chrome plated standard drill chucks to increase their life. When the chuck key, a simple device that tightens the chuck onto the bit, proved too small and cumbersome for use by a diver under limited visibility wearing restrictive diving gear and heavy gloves, designers responded by welding a 6-inch (15-cm) stem onto the key (Kenney 1972). This modification may have allowed the chuck to be tightened, but it did not solve the real problem—which was providing a quick change capability under conditions of limited dexterity. Fortunately, although primarily due to the cost of having an expensive submersible or diver in the water, underwater-tool designers are beginning to have both the foresight and the required funding to determine the real objective of an operation, and to provide specialized equipment to meet the objective.

For the purposes of this book, diving systems must be distinguished from work systems. A diving system is the total equipment necessary to bring a diver or a manipulator to a specific depth, to provide life support to the diver or bottom time to the submersible, and to return the diver or the submersible to the surface. A work system is the equipment added to the diver or to the submersible to allow or enhance the capability to do work. Without a work system, a diver or a submersible is primarily only an observer.

This book is directed toward the design of work systems. Information concerning diving systems is limited to the characteristics and capabilities of diving systems that are most pertinent to the design of work systems.

DIVER AND MANIPULATOR CHARACTERISTICS

THE characteristics of both divers and manipulators that are directly related to the performance of work underwater are discussed in this chapter. The information included is not exhaustive, but is intended to provide sufficient background for understanding the influence of each characteristic on work system design. The discussion of diver characteristics is somewhat brief; more detailed discussions of the physiological and psychological aspects of the diver can be found in books by such authors as J.B. MacInnis, S. Miles, C.J. Lambertsen, and D.L. Beckman, and in the U.S. Navy Diving Manual. The design and performance characteristics of manipulators are covered in greater detail.

DIVER CAPABILITIES AND LIMITATIONS

The use of divers to perform underwater work provides on-the-spot judgment and adaptability to unexpected conditions that cannot be provided in any other manner. This is particularly true when conventional manually operated surface tools are used for an underwater task. However, the near weightlessness and difficult movement, the often restricted visibility, and the low water temperatures often encountered create physical and psychological stresses that must be considered in tool design. Also, in many cases, limited bottom must be considered. Simple underwater tasks of brief duration in shallow water may result in little physical degradation with respect to surface work, but more demanding underwater tasks can result in disproportionate degradation of performance (Hackman 1967).

Effects of Weightlessness

The human body has nearly the same density as water; by inflating or deflating his lungs, a diver can generally become slightly buoyant or slightly negative. However, the selection of diving equipment, including breathing apparatus and thermal protection, as well as the depth of the dive influence a diver's buoyancy. Although the ability of a diver to control his buoyancy allows him mobility in three dimensions, this near weightlessness can severely limit his ability to perform certain tasks. The basic strength of a diver is little affected by depth; a man standing or sitting with back support can push with a force of about 50 lbf (220 N) either in or out of water. This and other limits are illustrated in Figure 1-1. Underwater tests by the authors, however, have indicated serious degradation in the ability of a diver—either free swimming or standing on the bottom—to do useful work or even to apply reaction forces to a powered tool. These tests indicate that a diver standing on the bottom of a tank can push with a force of only 6 or 7 lbf (27 or 31 N) and that the force must be directed so that little or no turning moments are applied to the body. If a diver holds an off-center handle with one hand and pushes a drill, for instance, with the other, his body will be rotated away from the drill. Because a free-swimming or free-standing diver can furnish only small reaction forces and torques, serious limitations should be expected in the operations he can perform without support, either for himself or for the tool. Examples of how the serious limitations to a diver due to weightlessness have been solved include anchoring the diver or the tool (see Figure 1-2), and eliminating or minimizing the reaction force, as is accomplished with impact tools (see Figure 1-3).

Resistance to Motion

Although the density of water provides a diver with a three-dimensional motion capability, it restricts his ability to move himself or his tools as quickly as he could in air. At a given velocity, for instance, the drag of a hammer in water is more than 800 times as great as that in air solely

Arm Forces Sitting

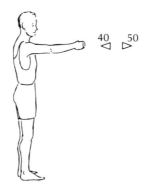

Arm Forces Standing

FIGURE 1-1   Human strength in lbf (Data from Dreyfuss, 1960.)

because of the density of the water. As mentioned in the Introduction, motions such as hammer blows are further attenuated because of the increased viscosity of the water in the impact zone.

Drag on a diver due to currents, gas supply and communications umbilicals, and the stiffness of diving suits also decreases his ability to move quickly in water. Typical diving equipment is fairly neutrally buoyant in water, but its weight out of water ranges from about 60 lb (27 kg) for typical self-contained underwater breathing apparatus (SCUBA) to as much as 250 lb (113 kg) for a helium-type, deep-sea hard hat suit (Myers, Holm, and McAllister 1969). Although the equipment can be nearly neutral in water, the size of the equipment and the effects of inertia on movement can severely restrict a diver's motion, especially into cramped spaces.

Restricted Visibility

In clear water with sufficient light, the optical properties of water alter a diver's perception of the size, color, and distance of objects. Since this is a

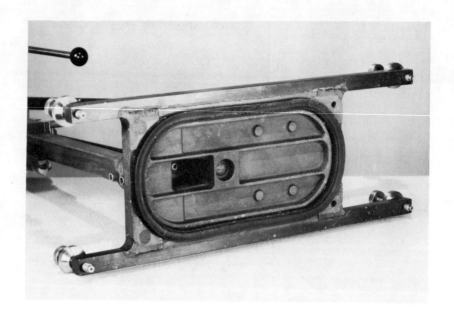

FIGURE 1-2   Suction base of underwater drill press used for providing reaction forces.

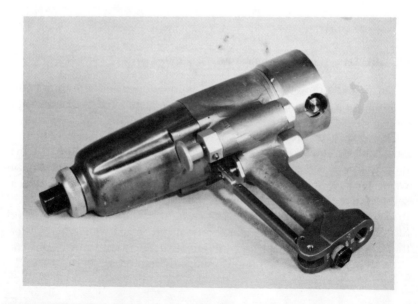

FIGURE 1-3   Typical diver-held impact tool.

constant phenomenon, divers quickly adapt to these characteristics. However, insufficient light due to depth or suspended particles can greatly degrade performance when a diver uses certain tools as well as cause safety hazards when he works in a hazardous area. In addition, a diver's mask or helmet may severely restrict his field of view. All of these characteristics must be considered in developing tools, especially tools that require assembly underwater or that require the reading of gauges or dials.

Limited Bottom Time

A diver's bottom time at depths beyond about 30 ft (9 m) or in cold water can be severely restricted unless sophisticated and costly saturation diving techniques or heated diving suits are used. Thus, it is important in developing a work system to match a diver's work requirements with his available bottom time.

Low Water Temperature

The world's oceans range in temperature from 28 to 86°F (−2 to +30°C); divers most commonly are exposed to water temperatures in the range of 41 to 59°F (5 to 15°C) (Myers, Holm, and McAllister 1969). Low water temperatures present significant problems for the work system designer. In addition to its potential effects on tool performance, cold water can severely restrict a diver's dexterity, coordination, and judgment. Therefore, where possible, tools should be designed such that mittened hands can perform all necessary tasks. When manual dexterity is needed in an underwater task, the difficulty of providing effective insulation to the hands and fingers can result in limited bottom time.

General Design Guidelines for Diver Tools

Tools designed for use by divers should be as small as possible to facilitate handling and to minimize current drag, but should be nearly neutral in water (which may require careful placement of flotation materials). Many divers have stated that, although they want a tool to be light in water, they prefer one that is 2 to 4 lb (.9 to 1.8 kg) in water over one that is neutral or that has a few pounds of positive buoyancy. Although it is not desirable to have umbilicals to diver tools, if an umbilical is necessary, it should be flexible and nearly neutral within the first few feet of the tool. It is especially important for tethered divers (those with gas supply, hot water, and/or communications lines) that the tool allow one-handed operation and handling, thereby leaving the diver a free hand for making suit and umbilical adjustments and for steadying himself and the tool in a current. Also, if the work is to be accomplished in a current or in limited visibility, the diver should not be required to make gage or dial readings in addition to accurately placing a tool; cloudy water and strong currents lead to inaccurate readings.

To help maximize a diver's effectiveness, his tools must be designed with switches and controls that are large enough to be manipulated with a gloved hand, and located so that they cannot be moved accidentally. Handles should be designed to resist hand slippage and to allow the diver to grip the tool with minimal cramping. An example of a design detail that can reduce a diver's work efficiency is the screw-type chuck found on most conventional power tools. This device is difficult for divers to manipulate when inserting or removing bits, cutters, and other accessories. An improved design employs square-shanked accessories that can be snapped into or removed from the tool quickly and easily (Hackman 1969).

It should be noted that strict adherence to one of these design guidelines may exclude adherence to others. Minimizing in-water tool weight, for instance, may require the addition of flotation materials, resulting in increased size. When such a conflict occurs, one-hand operation and the tool weight in water are usually the more important considerations.

MANIPULATORS

A manipulator is a device that can place a tool or other device (such as a grabber jaw) in the proper position to perform a task. The manipulator is usually considered the heart of the work system on submersibles; without it, a submersible is merely an observation platform. Special-purpose manipulators have been developed to provide the capability to do work at ocean depths greater than those at which divers can work and to perform certain tasks more expediently than divers.

Underwater manipulators, which have evolved from the nuclear remote-handling technologies, have only recently become a viable technology with standard, general-purpose underwater manipulators commercially available. Underwater manipulators may be mounted to submersibles (both manned and unmanned), diving bells, drill strings, and other underwater platforms. According to Busby (1976), 80 percent of all manned submersibles and 50 percent of all unmanned submersibles have at least one manipulator. Many submersibles have two manipulators, and the U.S. Navy's Work Systems Package (WSP), which can be attached to several submersibles (Wernli 1979, 1980; Wernli et al. 1978), has three manipulators. Although a majority of remote undersea tasks theoretically can be performed using one manipulator, a second or third manipulator often is needed to assist in holding the submersible or the object stable during the work. Maintaining a stable work platform is a major problem for small free-swimming vehicles. Any force or torque applied by a manipulator or by a tool held by a manipulator can upset the stability of a vehicle if it is not sitting on the bottom or firmly attached to the work object; in nonuniform work and loading, it may be impossible to maintain a vehicle's trim.

Many types of tools have been used to extend a manipulator's capability. In general, manipulators with a minimum of 6 degrees of freedom (six independent motions) are required to position a tool with respect to the work object. Manipulators mounted on undersea vehicles usually are mounted in one position and produce a series of arc motions about pivot points. Typical manipulators used to date for general underwater applications have approximately 100 lbf (445 N) capacity in any direction at their terminal device when fully extended. Most manipulators have an active length of 4 to 6 ft (1.3 to 2 m), and many are modeled to some extent after the human arm. Because of poor manipulator dexterity, experience has shown that performing a given task may take many times longer with a manipulator than with an unaided hand.

Manipulators may be hand powered, such as the master/slave manipulators used in the nuclear industry, or may be powered by auxiliary electrical or hydraulic power sources. For hand-powered manipulators, the slave arm position is usually controlled via mechanical linkages such that it exactly follows the master arm position. Very simple hand-powered arms were used on a few early, shallow-water manned submersibles, but were abandoned in later submersibles because of the limited operating space available within the personnel compartment to operate the arm, and because of problems in providing leak-free, low-friction hull penetrations. Therefore, only manipulators utilizing auxiliary power sources are considered in this section. In addition, present commercially available undersea manipulators are limited to hydraulic-powered units. Thus, although a significant portion of the following discussion is directly applicable to electric-powered manipulators, it is specifically directed to hydraulic-powered manipulators.

Manipulator Types

Manipulators can be categorized into two broad types: rate-control manipulators and position-control manipulators. In a rate-control manipulator, the motion actuators move at a fixed or controlled rate when a switch is actuated. This type of control often is accomplished with a simple switch (often a toggle or push-button type) directly controlling a simple solenoid-actuated valve. In a position-control manipulator, a slave arm follows exactly the position of a master unit. The master unit may be kinematically similar (but usually much smaller) to the slave arm or may consist of a nonsimilar device in which motion of the terminal portion of the master arm causes a directly proportional movement of the slave arm.

Several variations of each basic type of manipulator have been used. The control switches of a rate-control manipulator often are incorporated into a ''joy stick'' such that the movement of one control lever controls several motions. A simple computer circuit or servovalves can be used to make the speed of the actuators of a rate-control manipulator proportional to the switch or joy stick position. A capability of limiting the force in one or more motions by controlling the pressure to an actuator also can be added to a rate-control manipulator, and the U.S. Navy (Wernli 1979, 1980; Wernli et al. 1978) and several universities have experimented with preprogramming repetitive motions of both rate-control and position-control manipulators.

The reaction forces from touching or lifting objects can be sensed and fed back to the operator. On the sophisticated Diver Equivalent Manipulator System (DEMS) manipulator developed by General Electric (see Figure 1-4), the forces exerted by the slave actuators are sensed and used

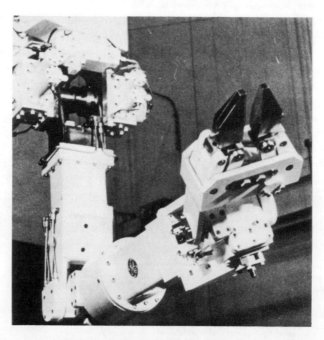

FIGURE 1-4   Diver Equivalent Manipulator System. (Courtesy of General Electric Co., King of Prussia, Pennsylvania.)

by the master arm to produce scaled-down forces that provide the operator with a sense of feel in all six axes of motion. This force feedback augments the visual feedback necessary to perform discrete tasks. The DEMS manipulator is a position-control manipulator in which the master arm is kinematically similar (spatially correspondent) to the slave arm.

A load (force) on the slave arm of the General Electric force-feedback manipulator requires a hydraulic pressure in the actuator proportional to the load. This pressure is sensed and a voltage signal proportional to the pressure is fed back through amplifier circuits to the equivalent electrically powered actuator of the master, which produces a force that is felt by the operator. When the operator moves the master arm, the resulting position error causes the slave actuator to move the slave arm in the same direction. The pressure in the slave actuator required to do this is fed back to the master actuator to produce a force that resists the operator's motion. Thus, the operator "feels" the inertia load. If the slave contacts a fixed object, the actuator pressure will rise suddenly, causing the master force also to rise suddenly, which will give the operator the "feeling" of contacting an object.

Other methods used to provide force feedback have included sensing actuator forces or torques with appropriately placed strain gages and using the resulting voltage to control servovalves (Uhrich 1977). Instead of providing feedback forces via a master arm, the force signals can be visually displayed, allowing use with either a position-control or a rate-control manipulator.

Advantages and Limitations of Various Manipulator Types

Early underwater manipulators were rate-control manipulators. For pick and place types of tasks like collecting bottom samples and debris, rate-control manipulators require as much as 100 times the time a man would require to perform a task (Myers, Holm, and McAllister 1969). For these types of operations, speed is more important than positioning accuracy. Position-control manipulators were developed to increase the speed of manipulator operations. In general, they require less time than rate-control manipulators to perform such tasks as picking up objects from the sea floor and placing them in a basket or acquiring a tool from a toolbox and moving the tool to a work area. Table 1-1 illustrates the individual joint motions that can be involved in doing a typical underwater task. These data were taken by the authors using the rate-control manipulator on the U.S. Navy's Work Systems Package (Caudy and Hackman 1977). The Work Systems Package has a toolbox that has individual underwater acquirable tools with underwater interchangeable toolbits. Note that the data in Table 1-1 begin with the tool already acquired by the manipulator—a process which

TABLE 1-1. Number of individual motions of rate-control manipulator joints required to perform a task.

				Task				
	Move to bit holder[a]	Acquire bit[b]	Move to work area	Engage tool	Perform typical task[c]	Move to bit holder	Return bit[b]	Move to tool holder	Place tool in holder
High speed rotary	4	5	6	4	3	10	15	7	15
Low speed rotary	7	7	6	9	4	11	6	7	11
Impact wrench	6	10	6	1	5	17	10	4	7
Rope knife	—	—	5	2	2	—	—	13	7
Chipping hammer	—	—	5	1	6	—	—	7	7
Spreader	—	—	12	8	2	—	—	12	14
Jack	—	—	6	2	3	—	—	13	1
Cable cutter	—	—	6	13	3	—	—	13	14
Explosive cable cutter	—	—	5	2	1	—	—	13	6
Explosive padeye	—	—	8	1	1	—	—	9	1
Average	6	7	7	4	3	13	10	10	8

a. Initial position was with tool acquired and retracted from toolbox.
b. Number of motions was highly dependent on bit location. It was much easier to acquire and return bits on the top center of the box.
c. Includes operations of the tool control switch, but does not include motion operations for such operations as wire brushing and grinding.

itself may require 10 to 20 individual joint motions. Thus, a typical work sequence can involve as many as 100 individual switch motions. Position-control manipulators typically eliminate all of the switch motions except for the jaw motion and tool control switches.

Once a tool is acquired and moved to the work area, the actual operation of the tool can involve slow, tedious motions. For instance, using an abrasive saw to make a 10-inch-long (25 cm) cut in ½-inch-thick (1.3 cm) steel plate would require 20 minutes of precise locating. For such operations, it is desirable to be able to concentrate on only one or two motions. For this reason, a switch-control option is usually added to even the most sophisticated position-control manipulators.

Table 1-2 lists typical tool operations conducted by manipulators and categorizes types and numbers of manipulator motions required during the actual working portion of the tool use. A position-control or a position-control force-feedback manipulator will improve tool operational time on those tasks requiring nonlinear motion after contact; it may or may not improve operation time for tools requiring no motion or essentially linear motion after contact. For operations where direct feed or simple angular motion about one joint is required, a rate-control manipulator may be easier to use during the actual tool operation because the operator can leave all of the joints stationary except the one being used. During such an operation in which a position-control manipulator is used, the operator must hold the master (and thus his own arm) in a fixed position for many minutes, which can be very tiring. Thus, as mentioned above, for position-control manipulators it is desirable to have a joint lock-out or switch control feature so that the manipulator can be operated in a rate-type mode once the tool is in position.

TABLE 1-2. Characteristic tool motions.

Task	Motion after Contact[a]	Number of Simultaneous Motion Directions Required[b]
Drill	Linear	1–2
Abrasive saw	Linear	1–2
Grind surface	Nonlinear	2–3
Brush surface	Nonlinear	2–3
Wrench	Linear	1–2
Knife	None	0
Chipping hammer cut	Linear	1–2
Surface cleaning	Nonlinear	2–3
Cable cutter	None	0
Jack or spreader	None	0

a.   The manner in which the tool would normally be moved after it is in contact with the work surface.

b.   Assumes that the platform is rigidly attached to the work piece.

A typical underwater work mission can involve several hours of manipulator operations. Table 1-3 summarizes the times that can be involved in a few typical missions excluding the time involved in transiting to and locating the work object. The values in Table 1-3 are for a rate-control manipulator with an experienced operator, and serve to emphasize that manipulator operation is a long, tedious job in real-work situations. Tests have shown that an inexperienced operator using a position-control manipulator can quickly perform tasks that would be very time-consuming for an inexperienced operator using a rate-control manipulator (Caudy and Hackman 1976). Experienced operators of rate-control manipulators reach a level of training in which they can move several joints at once and can perform many work scenarios with rate-type manipulators nearly as fast as they can be performed with position-control manipulators. Wernli (1979) presents a typical learning curve in which the experienced operator of a rate-control manipulator is 3 to 5 times faster than the inexperienced operator in typical work trials. For repetitive tasks such as tool exchange, the experienced operator is often more than 10 times faster than the inexperienced operator. The experience of the operator, therefore, often can be the determining factor in whether a job can or cannot be accomplished with a rate-control manipulator.

For repetitive tasks such as tool exchange, the speed of operation of a rate-control manipulator can be increased by attaching a position transducer to each actuator of a manipulator and feeding the actuator position back to a microprocessor that is programmed to move the manipulator through a specific set of motions. This modification was made on an experimental basis to the rate-control manipulator on the U.S. Navy's Work Systems Package (Wernli 1978) and was found to (1) reduce the time required for such repeatable functions as acquiring tools and related equipment, (2) greatly increase the operational accuracy of repeated op-

TABLE 1-3.   Manipulator and tool operation time involved in typical work mission. (Summarized from data in Wernli et al., 1978.)

Mission Description	Total Work Time (minutes)
Cut a 3 × 3-ft opening in $^3/_{32}$-inch-thick aluminum using an abrasive saw, spreader, and jack	216
Cut away a lock and two hinges on a ¼-inch-thick steel door using a drill, abrasive saw, and chipping hammer	265
Rig a hawser and cut and remove six tangled cables	65
Close four large gate valves (3 turns each)	46
Remove a flight recorder from an intact aircraft	79

erations, and (3) reduce operator workload and fatigue (Wernli 1978). The Work Systems Package has a toolbox with hydraulic-powered tools and interchangeable toolbits. In a typical work sequence, the manipulator would pick up a tool and attach a bit, perform the work, and return the bit and then the tool to their previous locations. Table 1-4 summarizes the results obtained. Based upon these results, it was estimated that the programmer could reduce the manipulator operating time for a typical work mission by 18 percent while relieving the operator of some of the more critical tasks (Wernli et al. 1978). A similar type of control can be used for positioning the camera that views the operation so that it will automatically follow the manipulator position. This control, which would relieve the operator of the need to reposition the camera as often, was estimated to save an average of 8 percent of the operating time for submersibles in which all manipulator operations must be viewed via television cameras.

Underwater tasks that fully utilize the unique capability of a force-feedback manipulator are those that require force control or force compliance, such as a task in which severe lateral forces caused by misalignment can break a tool (drilling and tapping are examples). To illustrate the degree to which the performance of a standard task could be improved by using a force-feedback system, a series of tests were performed by General Electric with a television system that could be controlled to permit varying degrees of visibility. Table 1-5 shows that force feedback increased the ease with which the known tasks could be performed in poor visibility compared to using the same system without force feedback, and that degradation of performance is much more rapid without force feedback. These experiments demonstrate that even with position control and force feedback, vision is the primary mode of operator feedback, and that cues provided by force feedback are secondary. If visibility deteriorates to the point that force feedback becomes the only mode of feedback, it may be possible to perform tasks that otherwise would be impossible.

Studies have shown that visually displayed feedback can result in less

TABLE 1-4   Reduction of rate-control manipulator task times by preprogrammed motions. (Summarized from data in Wernli et al. 1978.)

Task	Task Time (minutes) Experienced Operator	Programmer	Percent Reduction
Acquire tool	2.12	0.90	57
Replace tool	1.42	1.31	8
Acquire bit	1.23	1.00	17
Replace bit	1.30	0.74	43

TABLE 1-5   Results of underwater task performance using a position-control manipulator with and without force feedback (flanged pipe disassembly). (Data courtesy of General Electric Co., King of Prussia, Pennsylvania.)

Viewing Conditions	Average Task Cycle Time (seconds)	
	With FFB	Without FFB
Good	88	122
Fair	130	236
Poor	251	573
Zero	1180	Impossible

damaging force on tools, fewer task aborts, and less damage to a manipulator (Winget et al. 1977). However, while force feedback may reduce task performance times in master-slave-type arms, the use of visual feedback display results in increased task completion time because the operator must share his time between the displays and the work surface.

FIGURE 1-5   PaR Systems Corp. underwater manipulator. (Courtesy of PaR Systems Corp., St. Paul, Minnesota.)

Manipulators that offer a linear extend capability and direct rotation about the axis of the jaws (wrist rotate) have an advantage for some tool operations, such as drilling, sawing, torch feeding, and nut removal. Some rate-type manipulators, such as the PaR Systems Corporation manipulator (Figure 1-5), the Perry Ocean Products manipulator (Figure 1-6), and the Bruker manipulator (Figure 1-7), have a wrist-rotate feature. The PaR, Perry, and Bruker manipulators also have a linear extend capability, although it is not necessarily directly in line with the axis of the wrist. This extend capability would be ideal for such tool uses as drilling. The PaR arm linear extension requires the simultaneous movement of three rotary motions, which is known as cross-coupling, and which is not as desirable as pure sliding linear extension. The GE manipulator in Figure 1-4 (a force-feedback position-control manipulator) has neither a linear extension capability nor a direct rotation capability without moving more than one joint simultaneously. Theoretically, however, this is not a problem for a position-control manipulator. If the master is moved in a rotary motion or in a straight line, the slave will follow. In practice, however, for small, intricate motions it can be difficult to move 2 or 3 joints smoothly at one time.

The capability of a manipulator to make small, intricate motions will be

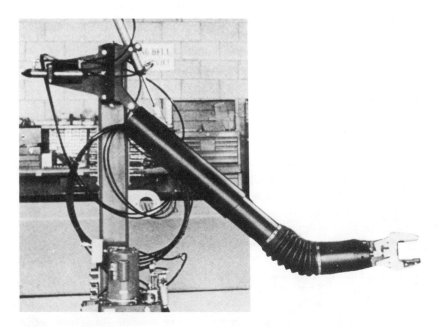

FIGURE 1-6   Perry Ocean Products six-function manipulator. (Courtesy of Perry Oceanographics, Inc., Riviera Beach, Florida.)

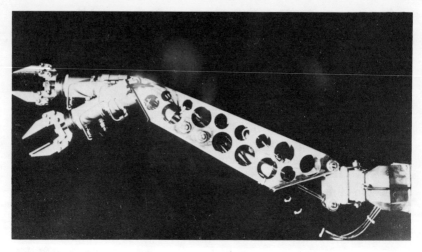

FIGURE 1-7 Bruker manipulator. (Courtesy of Bruker Ocean Technology Inc., Billerica, Massachusetts.)

of no avail if the submersible to which it is mounted continually makes erratic motions while the operator is attempting to do work. This is often the case with small, free-swimming submersibles. Even on a larger manned submersible, the vehicle's pitch and roll motions due to the normal manipulator arm motions can result in positioning errors at the manipulator's terminal device in excess of one inch (2.54 cm) (Myers, Holm, and McAllister 1969). However, the work function accuracy of an attached or bottom-sitting submersible may be limited only by the accuracy of the manipulator itself. One system, the U.S. Navy's Work Systems Package, uses two heavy-duty, 6-degree-of-freedom ''grabber'' arms (see Figure 1-8) to grasp the work object and stabilize the submersible. Force-feedback position-control manipulators such as the GE manipulator do offer an advantage over rate-control manipulators in situations where the vehicle cannot be positioned rigidly with respect to the work: the force-feedback position-control manipulator allows the operator to comply with the vehicle motion more readily.

Rate-control manipulators often have an advantage over position-control manipulators in their operating envelope (the volume of space in which the manipulator can perform work with respect to its mounting location). Figures 1-9a and 1-9b show the operating envelope for the General Electric DEMS manipulator (a position-control type) and Figure 1-10 shows the operating envelope for the PaR manipulator (a rate-control type). It is easier to incorporate a large operating envelope in a rate-control manipulator than in a position-control unit. The manipulator arm of a position-control unit in general cannot have the joint actuator locations

FIGURE 1-8   U.S. Navy's Work Systems Package grabber arm.

and joint motion capability designed such that the middle actuator of three rotary joints can come in alignment and operate to either side of this alignment. For instance, the elbow joint of a shoulder- elbow- wrist combination cannot pivot such that all three joints can come into alignment. This joint alignment will cause a statically indeterminent state for a kinematically similar master arm. Also, such so-called "degenerative positions" cause forces to be transferred purely mechanically to the vehicle, limiting the ability to sense the force in a force-feedback manipulator. This operating envelope limitation is not a problem for rate-control nonforce-feedback manipulators where all forces are transferred purely mechanically to the vehicle.

In addition to actuator design, the master control unit can influence the operating envelope. Any limitation to the operating envelope of the master arm can directly affect the operating envelope of the slave arm. This envelope limitation is especially important for use in the pilot's compartment of a small manned submersible where it may be difficult to find room to operate a master arm. With a small control box, the operator can move about the compartment and, if necessary, use the control while viewing the

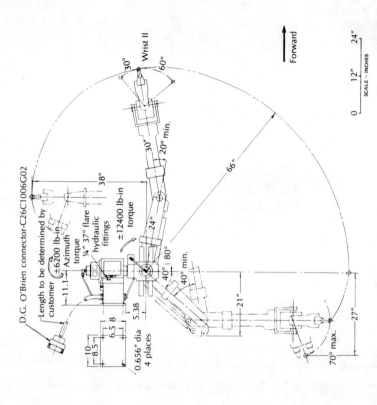

FIGURE 1-9a General Electric DEMS manipulator operating envelope, side view. (Courtesy of General Electric Company, King of Prussia, Pennsylvania.)

20

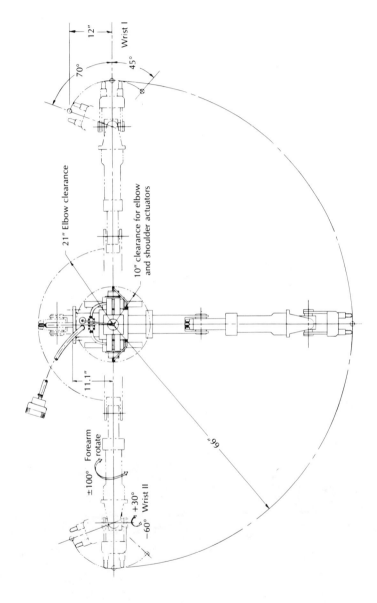

FIGURE 1-9b General Electric DEMS manipulator operating envelope, plan view. (Courtesy of General Electric Company, King of Prussia, Pennsylvania.)

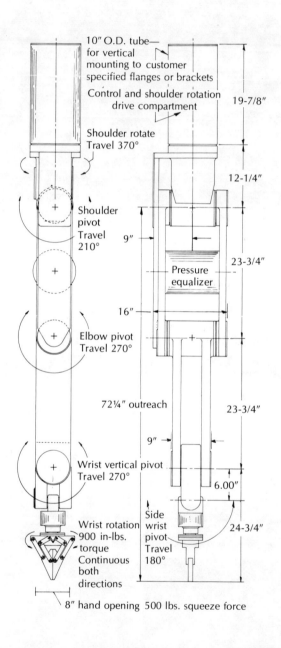

10" O.D. tube— for vertical mounting to customer specified flanges or brackets

Control and shoulder rotation drive compartment

19-7/8"

Shoulder rotate Travel 370°

12-1/4"

Shoulder pivot Travel 210°

9"

Pressure equalizer

23-3/4"

16"

Elbow pivot Travel 270°

72¼" outreach

23-3/4"

9"

Wrist vertical pivot Travel 270°

6.00"

Wrist rotation 900 in-lbs. torque Continuous both directions

Side wrist pivot Travel 180°

24-3/4"

8" hand opening 500 lbs. squeeze force

FIGURE 1-10   PaR Systems Corp. underwater manipulator operating envelope. (Courtesy of PaR Systems Corp., St. Paul, Minnesota.)

operation from a viewport. In many manned submersibles, using a position-control manipulator will limit the operator to camera viewing only.

The manner in which the manipulator arm must be attached to the submersible can also limit the operating envelope. The location of the submersible's strong points, lights, and viewports and/or cameras may dictate the final location of the manipulator and limit its operating envelope. In general, rate-control manipulators are easier to modify and adapt to specific submersibles than are position-control manipulators.

Position-control force-feedback manipulators are, by necessity, typically 4 to 7 times more expensive than rate-control manipulators of similar size. The cost of position-control manipulators without force feedback is intermediate to the two extremes. Because of their complexity, position-control manipulators are somewhat more prone to failure and somewhat more costly to repair than rate-control units. However, the increase in speed that a position-control unit may add to a task must be considered in the overall cost analysis. If the unit can save expensive submersible and ship time, the decreased manipulator reliability and increased costs may be outweighed by the overall cost savings.

Typical Manipulators

Table 1-6 compares the features of several underwater manipulators. The Hydro Products manipulator, the smallest unit, is designed specifically for use with a 4 × 3.5 × 4-ft (1.3 × 1.1 × 1.3-m) unmanned submersible. The remainder of the manipulators included in the table are more general-purpose units; all have in-water lift capabilities when fully extended in the 100 to 260 lbf (440 to 1200 N) range. The operating envelopes of the General Electric and PaR manipulators were shown in Figures 1-9a, 1-9b, and 1-10. Although a weight summary is included for comparison, it is difficult to compare weights directly because of the standard equipment. For instance, the Hydro Products manipulator has a built-in abrasive saw, the MBA Associates manipulator does not have general-purpose jaws, and the General Electric and PaR manipulators have all valving built into the arm.

The hydraulic flow rate requirements of the arms are all similar, although the requirements of the General Electric and the MBA Associates arms are somewhat greater than those of the others. Both are controlled by servovalves that characteristically have a leakage flow and are not as horsepower efficient as many solenoid control valves, especially zero-leakage types. This "leakage" horsepower is a very important consideration on energy-limited vehicles, such as battery-powered submersibles.

TABLE 1-6 Comparison of manipulators.

Features	Perry Five-Function	Perry Six-Function	General Electric	Programmed and Remote Systems	Hydro Products	Bruker	MBA Associates[l]	WSP Grabber
Type of control	Rate	Rate	Position/FFB	Rate	Rate	Rate	Semiposition	Rate
Overall length (inches)[a]	48.5	84.5	66	72.2	36	80[k]	60	108
Degrees of freedom	5	6	7	7	4	6	4	6
Weight (lb)[b,f]	65	90	200[j]	295[j]	16	154	146[k]	195
Load capability (lbf)[c,g]	150	150	100	100	30	264	150	250
Hydraulic requirements								
Flow, gpm[d]	1	1	2	1	0.3	1.6	4	1
Pressure, psi[e]	1000	1000	3000	1750–3000	2000	1500	2000	3000
Horizontal motion (degrees)[h]	90	115	180	370	None	240	180	130
Vertical motion (degrees)[h]	90	105	120	210	248	130	150	90
Linear extension (inches)[a]	10	18	(m)	(i)	None	24	18	24
Built-in jettison capability	No	No	No[m]	No	No	Yes	No	Yes

a. Multiple by 0.0254 to convert to meters.
b. Multiply by 0.454 to convert to kilograms.
c. Multiply by 4.45 to convert to Newtons.
d. Multiply by 0.0000631 to obtain m³/sec.
e. Multiply by 6895 to obtain Pascal (N/m²).
f. In water with oil fill, not including control valves unless noted.
g. Fully extended.

h. Actuator motion nearest the mounting base.
i. About 3 ft (0.9 m) linear extension along a line of action through wrist and shoulder pivots.
j. Weights include valve package.
k. From horizontal swing point.
l. Used on the SCARAB submersible constructed by Ametek Straza for underwater telephone-line repair.
m. Terminal extension can be linear up to about 30 inches depending on the operator.
n. Can be added as an option.

Few data are available concerning the positioning accuracy of underwater manipulators. Table 1-7 shows some typical data for the PaR manipulator and the Work Systems Package (WSP) grabbers (Caudy and Hackman 1977). These data are the minimum incremental motions measured at the tip of the extended manipulator that can easily be achieved by quick motions of the switch-controlled arms. By jogging the controls, it is possible to position the arms more closely. However, the key to accurate positioning is submersible stability and good vision of the operation. Usually the degree of visibility (especially the operator's depth perception) limits the accuracy of operation.

Specific Capabilities of Underwater Manipulators

Underwater manipulators often are modified for or designed for a specific application. The Hydro Products manipulator, for example, has a built-in abrasive saw that allows it to sever up to ¾-inch-diameter (1.9 cm) wire rope. It also has a synthetic rope cutter built into its grabber jaws for up to

TABLE 1-7   Typical minimum incremental motions for two rate-control manipulators.

	Typical Minimum Incremental Motion[a] (measured at finger tip of extended manipulator)	
	PaR Manipulator	WSP Grabber Manipulator
Shoulder up	1/2 inch[b]	3/8 inch
Shoulder down	1/2 inch	1/4 inch
Shoulder left	1 inch	—
Shoulder right	1 inch	—
Elbow up	1/8 inch	—
Elbow down	1/4 inch	—
Extend	3/16 inch	1/2 inch
Retract	3/16 inch	1/8 inch
Wrist up	3/8 inch	1 inch
Wrist down	1/2 inch	3/4 inch
Wrist left	1/4 inch	—
Wrist right	1/4 inch	—
Wrist clockwise	3°	1°
Wrist counterclockwise	3°	1°
Jaw open	1/2 inch	1/4 inch
Jaw closed	1/2 inch	1/8 inch

a. By trial and error using quick jogging motions of the switches it is possible to position more accurately.

b. Multiply by 2.54 to convert to cm.

¾-inch-diameter (1.9 cm) rope. These tools provide it with additional debris-clearing capability for working around wellhead re-entry cones. The General Electric and the PaR arms can be obtained with provisions for underwater mateable hydraulic tools, the advantages of which are discussed in the underwater tool section of this book. The General Electric arm also has underwater changeable jaws. As noted in Table 1-6, some manipulators also have a built-in jettison capability, which is desirable in case the manipulator becomes entangled in the work object or debris and cannot be freed.

Guidelines for Designing Underwater Manipulators

The following list contains guidelines for underwater manipulator design. Although this list is specifically directed toward manipulator design, it should be noted that the most important component of the system is the viewing system, which generally consists of television cameras, lights, and viewports. If the operator can see the work area well, he can do useful work with a simple manipulator. If the operator cannot see the work area or can only see it poorly, he has little chance of doing useful work with even the most sophisticated manipulator.

1. A well-designed manipulator will be large at the shoulder and small at the hand. This design puts the bending strength and maximum stiffness where needed, holds down the unnecessary moments caused by excess weight at large distances from the shoulder, helps keeps the natural frequency of the arm high, and provides increased visibility.

2. The wrists of the manipulator should be small and the fingers should be long such that the finger operation can easily be viewed during delicate operations such as tool change, and such that the fingers can get near and fit into small places. Large wrists and small fingers severely limit the ability to view delicate work and tool exchange with a television camera.

3. The manipulator fingers must have accurate position control. It is important to be able to stop, hold, and move the fingers in small, easily controllable increments.

4. Position-control manipulators can save time over rate-control manipulators in getting from one work area to another, especially if visibility is good. In poor visibility, force feedback as well as position control can save time.

5. Position-control manipulators, even if counterweighted, can tire

the operator quickly for delicate work because of the necessity of holding his hand in a given position for extended periods. This problem can be alleviated by providing lock-outs on each function so that the operator can concentrate on one joint for small movements. A quick-position lock for the entire manipulator master is very helpful to the operator in maintaining a fixed position.

6. If multiple-position-control manipulators are to be used, a quick-position lock for the entire manipulator master is essential because at times it will be necessary for the operator to use both hands to operate one manipulator.

7. Cross coupling between motions may impair delicate work. To minimize cross coupling, make the centerlines of universal joint motions, such as in the wrist and shoulder, intersect, and make the wrist-to-terminal-device distance as short as possible. In addition, wherever possible, eliminate the need to move two or more joints to make a single motion that must be repeated often.

8. The manipulator fingers should have "feel" to aid in determining where the interferences or tight fits are for delicate operations such as tool exchange. The "feel" may be force feedback or, more simply, finger contact or tool alignment indicators, but it is essential for accurate tool exchange.

9. For a rate-control manipulator, it is important that the rate of motion be slow enough for accurate positioning of the manipulator. Tests have shown that operators generally select a maximum rate of 4 inch/s (10 cm/s), even for gross manipulator motions.

10. The manipulator fingers should be a light color for visibility. Gray is preferrable to white because white can cause a bloom that fuzzes the edge of the manipulator. Illumination of the fingers with a light in the wrist could aid in delicate work, such as tool removal.

11. Where possible, the manipulator fingers should be smooth with a minimum of sharp edges to prevent cutting or damaging tools.

12. The limits of motion of the manipulator should not be limited by the limits of motion of the operator's hand and arms. The operator will stand, kneel, lean, or do whatever is necessary to complete the task if the motion capability is available.

UNDERWATER TOOLS

TOOLS are used to extend the useful work capability of both divers and manipulators. Tools that receive all of the energy required to perform a task from a diver or manipulator are referred to as hand tools. Tools that utilize energy in addition to that supplied by the operator are referred to as power tools. To date, most underwater tools are adaptations of tools used to perform similar tasks on land. Recently, however, a number of tools have been designed specifically for use underwater, and ocean engineers are now treating the diver/tool combination and the submersible/manipulator/tool combination as a system. An example of how this has been done for manipulator/tool work systems is the Work Systems Package developed for use with the U.S. Navy's Pontoon Implacement Vehicle (PIV), CURV III, RUWS, Alvin, Sea Cliff, and Turtle vehicles (Hackman et al. 1975; Uhler 1976; Wernli 1978, 1980). Incorporating the Work Systems Package tool system expands the capabilities of any of the vehicles beyond basic observation and inspection to more sophisticated work tasks. The tools, which include impact wrenches, abrasive saws, rope knives, chipping hammers, spreaders, jacks, and cable cutters, are designed for operation at depths reaching 20,000 ft (6100 m).

The Work Systems Package has been used on the PIV, CURV III, and RUWS (all unmanned submersibles) to demonstrate that a submersible can carry an entire tool shop to the bottom and complete a variety of jobs without returning to the surface. These tools are intended to do the work of a diver at great depths. Therefore, large tools are not included in the system. The tools provided are the type and size that would normally be used by a mechanic in performing field operations on land. The tool suit was selected on the basis of work functions required to perform typical underwater tasks encountered in salvage operations, such as debris clearance, hull penetration, and salvage-valve coupling attachment. The tools are divided into three categories: rotary, linear, and power velocity (explosively actuated). A list of the tools included on the Work Systems Package is shown in Table 2-1. The rotary and linear hydraulic tools all feature the capability of making the hydraulic connections when the manipulator acquires the tool and removes it from the toolbox (see Figure 2-1).

Examples of tools that have been designed specifically for underwater use are cited throughout the following sections. Because most of the work underway today involves the development of improved power tools, power tools will be covered in more detail than hand tools, with the discussion of hand tools being oriented more toward application than toward design.

FIGURE 2-1   U.S. Navy's Work Systems Package manipulator removing a tool from the toolbox.

TABLE 2-1 Summary of Work Systems Package tool suit.

Operating Mode	Power Head	Bits	Function	Capability
Rotary Hydraulic	High speed	Wire brush, Grinder, Cutoff wheel	Brush, Grind, Cut	125 lbf·in[a]
	Low speed	Drill, Tap, Die	Drill, Thread	275 lbf·in
	Reciprocating knife	—	Rope cut	2-inch dia.[b]
	Chipping hammer	Chisel	Chip	37 lbf, 21 strokes/s
	Impact wrench	Sockets	Bolt-unbolt	1,320 lbf·in
	Winch	—	Pull	1,000 lbf[c]
Linear Hydraulic	Jack	—	Jacking	19,000 lbf, 8-1/2 inch
	Spreader	—	Spreading	2,876 lbf, 13 inch
	Cable cutter	—	Cut cable	1-inch-dia. wire rope
Power Velocity	Cable cutter	—	Cut cable	1-1/4-inch-dia. wire rope
	Stud gun	Padeye	Attach padeye	1/8 to 5/8-inch-thick mild steel

a. Multiply by 0.113 to convert to N·m.
b. Multiply by 2.54 to convert to cm.
c. Multiply by 4.45 to convert to N.

HAND TOOLS

Table 2-2 lists typical diver-held hand tools and some of their uses. Nearly all of these tools, with the exception of the hammers, banding tools, taps, dies, and pipe cutters, have also been adapted for use by manipulators. Manipulators typically cannot attain the needed velocity with adequate controllability to perform hammering operations and, without the use of auxiliary power tools, usually lack the positioning accuracy, the strength, or the flexibility to use the other excluded tools.

Of the hand tools mentioned, the knife, pry bar, various saws and cutters, and rigging equipment are used the most frequently because a large portion of underwater work involves removing debris, recovering objects, and installing temporary patches. Of the saws, the hacksaw with an 18 to 22-teeth-per-inch blade is commonly used by divers because of its adaptability to various materials. Ordinary socket, box, and open wrenches are used by divers for bolting along with vise grip pliers and pipe wrenches where nuts or bolt heads are highly corroded or rounded off.

TABLE 2-2   Typical diver-operated hand tools and their uses.

Tool	Use
Banding tools	Securing forms for cutting and welding
Bolt cutter	Shear rods, spikes, pins, wires
Chisel	Cutting
C-clamps	Securing objects temporarily
Drill	Drilling holes in wood
File	Enlarging holes
Grappling hook	Securing objects, anchoring
Hack saw	Cutting steel cable, heavy ropes, small pipe
Hammer	
Carpenter	Driving nails, small pins
Chipping	Cleaning growth and scale off welds, taking rock samples
Sledge	Driving stakes, spikes, pins
Handsaw	Cutting plank, timbers, piling
Knife	Cutting light line, rope
Pipe cutter	Cutting pipe
Pry bar	Moving or removing objects
Scraper	Cleaning surfaces
Shears, snips, and side cutters	Cutting line, small wires
Shovel	Moving small amounts of bottom soil
Standard rigging	Securing and moving objects
Taps and dies	Threading pipe or rod
Wrench	Turning nuts, bolts, pipe fittings

Because of the problems of handling and losing tools underwater, divers usually carry the tools to the work site in a canvas bag, attach them to their diving belt with a lanyard, or attach them to a shackle and slide them down a descending line (Myers, Holm, and McAllister 1969). When used with manipulators, a hand tool is usually either clamped to the manipulator terminal device or provided with special adapters or brackets such that the manipulator can use its jaws to grasp the tool.

POWER TOOLS

Power tools can be classified according to their source of power, such as pneumatic, hydraulic, electric, or explosive. They also can be classified according to types of operating requirements, such as those operations requiring the breakdown and removal of material (e.g., drilling, sawing, chipping, brushing, grinding, and descaling), those operations requiring controlled forces or torques (e.g., nail driving, nut running, core driving, and winching), or those operations requiring the joining of material (e.g., welding and clamping). Another method of classification is based on the function of the tool, such as drilling, sawing, welding, or brushing. For this discussion, a method of classification midway between the latter two is used. Tools specifically designed for controlled forces are discussed first, followed by tools for mechanical cutting, mechanical cleaning, welding, nonmechanical cutting, and attachment. A more detailed discussion of the power sources for the tools is presented in a later section.

At present, a majority of the tools used by manipulators are hydraulically powered, while both pneumatic power and hydraulic power are extensively used for diver tools. Most commercially available pneumatic-powered and hydraulic-powered tools built for surface use can be used directly underwater to limited depths, although they must be cleaned and lubricated immediately after each use to reduce corrosion damage. Using surface tools at excessive depths without pressure compensation can damage seals and lead to serious leakage and/or degraded performance.

Controlled Force Tools

As Myers, Holm, and McAllister (1969) point out, successful tool handling systems must fulfill three criteria: "positioning, compliance, and reaction loops." The *positioning* criteria refer to the accuracy with which the tool can be located or oriented at a certain spot in space versus the final accuracy requirement of the task. For instance, if a manipulator has a positioning accuracy of ½ inch (1.3 cm) (see Table 1-7) and must place a socket on a nut with a clearance of 0.01 inch (0.025 cm), a means must be provided to guide the socket. *Compliance* is the ability of the handling system to relieve the forces caused by the positioning mismatch. The *reaction loop* refers to the path through which the forces generated by the tool are returned to the work piece. For instance, this path may be from the tool bit to the tool, to a manipulator arm, to a submersible, to a second manipulator or grabber arm, to the work piece.

A diver usually can easily handle the positioning and compliance requirements and often is called upon to complete the reaction loop. However, the general rule for both divers and manipulators is that whenever the reaction forces generated are significant, the reaction path should be kept within the tool. One method would be to have the tool transmit all of its reaction forces to the water (Hackman 1967, 1970). Another method, the so-called controlled force approach, is to design the tool so that either all of the reaction forces are transmitted directly back into the work object (see Figure 2-2) or the work forces are mitigated through the use of impact techniques such that the force transmitted to the tool operator is within the operator's reaction capability. Controlled force tools include rotary impact wrenches, linear impact hammers, jacks, spreaders, and many mechanical cutting devices.

FIGURE 2-2 Diver-operated drill press with suction attachment.

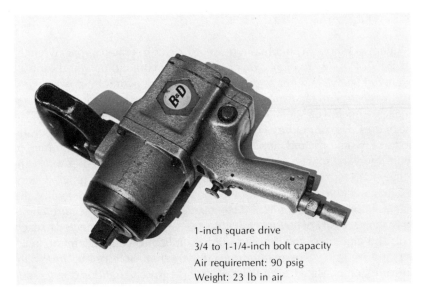

1-inch square drive
3/4 to 1-1/4-inch bolt capacity
Air requirement: 90 psig
Weight: 23 lb in air

FIGURE 2-3   Pneumatic-powered impact wrench.

3/4-inch square drive
5/8 to 3/4-inch bolt capacity
Weight: 10 lb in air
No-load speed: 950 rpm at 5 gpm
Hydraulic requirement: 5 gpm at
  1000 psig minimum

FIGURE 2-4   Lightweight, diver-operated, hydraulic-powered impact wrench.
(Courtesy of Stanley Hydraulic Tools, Milwaukie, Oregon.)

Figure 2-3 shows a pneumatic-powered, diver-operated impact wrench; Figure 2-4 a lightweight, diver-operated, hydraulic-powered impact wrench; Figure 2-5 a heavy-duty, diver-operated, hydraulic-powered impact wrench; and Figure 2-6 a manipulator-operated, hydraulic-powered impact wrench. The specific characteristics of each tool are summarized in the figures. The principle of the impact tool is to take small, steady torque or force reactions and apply them to the output shaft or hammer in short-interval impacts, so that increased momentary forces or torques are delivered to the output. The manipulator-operated impact wrench (Figure 2-6) has a feature that the hydraulic connections are completed when the manipulator acquires the tool (Hackman et al. 1975). This feature eliminates the necessity of having individual hydraulic hoses connected to each tool, and eliminates the problems of hydraulic hose entanglement, kinking, and snagging. The feature does require that each tool be internally pressure compensated such that external pressure variations due to sub-

1-1/2-inch square drive
1-1/2 to 2-inch bolts
Weight: 80 lb in air
No-load speed: 565 rpm
  at 16 gpm

Hydraulic requirement: 16 gpm at
1000 psig minimum

FIGURE 2-5   Heavy-duty, diver-operated, hydraulic-powered impact wrench. (Courtesy of Stanley Hydraulic Tools, Milwaukie, Oregon.)

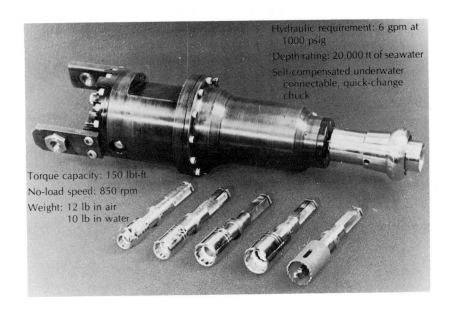

Hydraulic requirement: 6 gpm at 1000 psig

Depth rating: 20,000 ft of seawater

Self-compensated underwater connectable, quick-change chuck

Torque capacity: 150 lbf-ft
No-load speed: 850 rpm
Weight: 12 lb in air
        10 lb in water

FIGURE 2-6   Manipulator-operated, hydraulic-powered impact wrench.

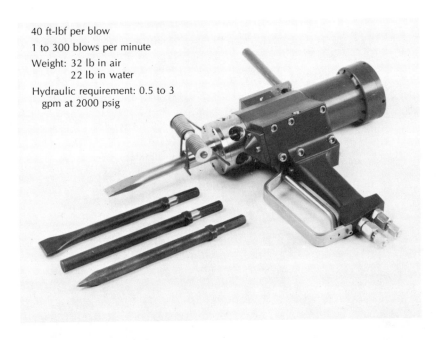

40 ft-lbf per blow
1 to 300 blows per minute
Weight: 32 lb in air
        22 lb in water
Hydraulic requirement: 0.5 to 3 gpm at 2000 psig

FIGURE 2-7   Diver-operated linear impact tool.

mersible depth changes will not damage the tool (a discussion of pressure compensation is presented in Chapter 4).

Figure 2-7 shows a diver-operated linear impact tool and Figure 2-8 shows a manipulator-operated chipping hammer. Both have a linear impact mechanism. The chipping hammer uses a rotary-motor-operated cam to raise a spring-loaded hammer and release it; it is very limited in its energy capacity per blow. The diver-operated tool operates on an oil-compression principle that allows an energy storage of 40 ft-lbf (54 J) per blow. Because it uses oil compression for energy storage, the tool is not depth sensitive as are pneumatic impact systems, such as those used in many pavement breakers, that must be restricted to shallow water usage.

Figure 2-9 shows a manipulator-operated, hydraulic-powered spreader. Similar tools are available for diver use (Mittleman 1978) and are operated either with a hand pump or with an auxiliary power supply. These tools are especially useful for tearing holes in light metal, for lifting objects, and for bending or straightening such items as propellors.

Mechanical Cutting Tools

Mechanical cutting tools are those tools that cause the breakdown, or the breakdown and removal, of material. Examples of mechanical cutting

Force capacity: 37 lbf at 1260 strokes per minute

Weight: 26 lb dry
　　　　21 lb wet

Hydraulic requirements: 2-1/2 gpm at 3000 psig

Depth rating: 20,000 ft

Self-compensated, underwater connectable

FIGURE 2-8　Manipulator-operated chipping hammer.

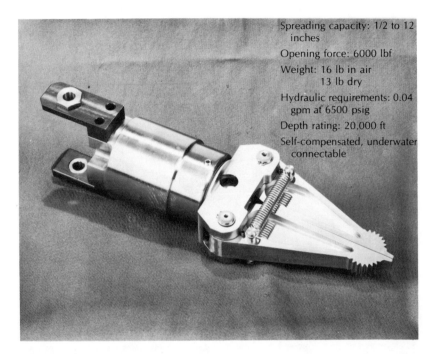

Spreading capacity: 1/2 to 12 inches

Opening force: 6000 lbf

Weight: 16 lb in air
13 lb dry

Hydraulic requirements: 0.04 gpm at 6500 psig

Depth rating: 20,000 ft

Self-compensated, underwater connectable

FIGURE 2-9   Manipulator-operated spreading tool.

operations include drilling, sawing, chipping, brushing, grinding, descaling, shearing, milling, and tapping. Of the many mechanical cutting tools available, probably the most versatile type is the rotary abrasive saw, which can be used to cut metals and nonmetals such as concrete, rubber, wood, and plastics. It is especially valuable in cutting composite materials, such as steel-reinforced rubber, where it will cut both materials. Figure 2-10 shows a diver-operated abrasive saw and Figure 2-11 shows a manipulator-operated abrasive saw.

Although abrasive saws are very versatile, they require considerable horsepower. Many reinforced abrasive cutoff wheels are rated by their manufacturers to cut best at 12,500 to 16,000 surface ft/min (63.5 to 81.3 m/s). Figure 2-12 shows the shaft speed required to provide the desired surface speed for various abrasive wheel diameters. High wheel speeds, however, result in very high viscous drag horsepower losses (and correspondingly high reaction torques) for wheels operating in water. In practice, underwater abrasive wheels are seldom operated at the recommended wheel surface speed because of the viscous losses. Figure 2-13 displays viscous drag data collected by the authors for various types of wheels operating in fresh water. The horsepower needed to perform the actual work must be added to the losses shown in Figure 2-13 to get the

Depth of cut: 3 inches   Wheel speed: 3500 rpm at 15 gpm
Wheel diameter: 10 inches   Hydraulic requirements: 15 gpm at
Weight: 19 lb in air   1500 psig

FIGURE 2-10 Diver-operated abrasive cutoff saw. (Courtesy of Stanley Hydraulic Tools, Milwaukie, Oregon.)

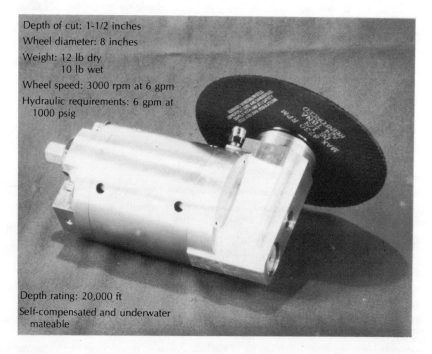

Depth of cut: 1-1/2 inches
Wheel diameter: 8 inches
Weight: 12 lb dry
        10 lb wet
Wheel speed: 3000 rpm at 6 gpm
Hydraulic requirements: 6 gpm at
   1000 psig

Depth rating: 20,000 ft
Self-compensated and underwater
   mateable

FIGURE 2-11 Manipulator-operated abrasive cutoff saw.

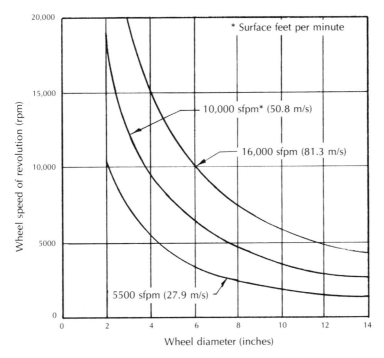

FIGURE 2-12 Grinding and abrasive wheel speed and diameter for various surface speeds.

total horsepower required. For instance, an 8.0-inch-diameter (20 cm) abrasive wheel was found to require an input of 5.3 hp (3950 W) to rotate freely at a speed of 2700 rpm in water and to require an input of 7.0 hp (5220 W) at 2700 rpm while under heavy cutting loads. Thus, only 25 percent of the energy input was going to useful work. In addition, the abrasive wheel was being operated well below its 7500 rpm rating, and it was estimated (by extrapolation) that an input power of 70 hp (52,200 W) would have been required to rotate the wheel at its design speed. Because of the tremendous viscous losses, the operating speed of abrasive wheels is usually a compromise between the cutting speed desired and the power available from acceptably sized motors and power supplies.

Other power cutting tools that are useful underwater include saber, chain, band, and reciprocating saws; shears; snips; cable cutters; and drills. Saber saws can be used underwater for cutting metals, plastics, and wood. Chain saws (see Figure 2-14) are frequently used for cutting pilings and thick wood. Band saws can be used for cutting metals and certain cables (CEL 1976) where the material being cut is not too hard and where the work material and saw can be held solidly enough to prevent binding. Band saws require a lower total power input than an abrasive saw to

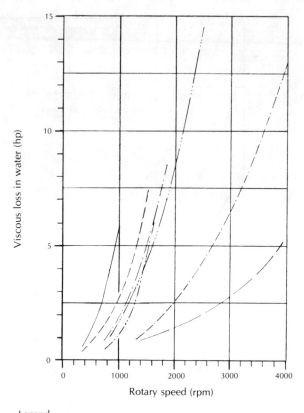

Legend

———————— 8-inch-dia x 3/4-inch-thick radial wire brush
— — — — 6-inch-dia. x 1-1/2-inch-thick radial wire brush
———·——— 6-inch-dia. x 5/8-inch-thick radial wire brush
———··——— 6-inch-dia. cup-wheel-type wire brush
———···——— 11-3/4-inch-dia. x 1/8-inch thick abrasive wheel
— —·— — 8-inch-dia. x 1/16-inch-thick abrasive wheel
— — — — 6-inch-dia. x 1/32-inch-thick abrasive wheel

FIGURE 2-13   Viscous horsepower losses for various wire brushes and abrasive
wheels rotating freely in water.

perform cutting jobs within their capability. Reciprocating saws are useful
for lighter work, especially in tight areas. Shear cutting can be done with
snips, nibblers, and power shears, but the application of these tools in
underwater work is somewhat limited because so much work at present is
salvage in which the metal is either too heavy for shear cutting or else it is
not possible for the jaws to reach both sides of the metal. Hydraulic-
powered cable and bar cutters are also used by divers (see Figure 2-15) and
with manipulators (see Figure 2-16). Drilling is used for making precision
holes up to 2 inches (5 cm) in diameter, although impact-driven mechanical punches are also available for less precise holes. Various shaped cuts

can also be made with shaped charges and liquid explosives, as will be discussed later.

So-called "velocity powered" or "ordnance actuated" cable and bar cutters are also used extensively underwater. These tools use the energy created from an explosive charge to drive the cutting blade with enough

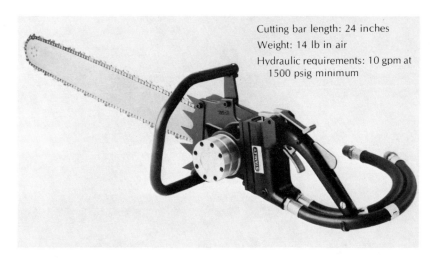

Cutting bar length: 24 inches
Weight: 14 lb in air
Hydraulic requirements: 10 gpm at 1500 psig minimum

FIGURE 2-14   Hydraulic-powered chain saw for diver use. (Courtesy of Stanley Hydraulic Tools, Milwaukie, Oregon.)

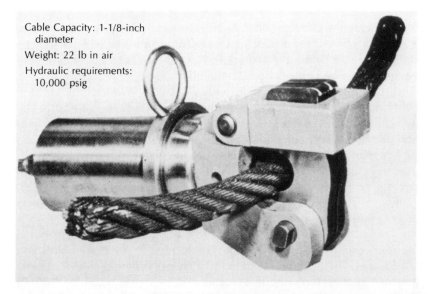

Cable Capacity: 1-1/8-inch diameter
Weight: 22 lb in air
Hydraulic requirements: 10,000 psig

FIGURE 2-15   Diver-operated, hydraulic-powered cable and bar cutter. (Courtesy of H. K. Porter Inc., Somerville, Massachusetts.)

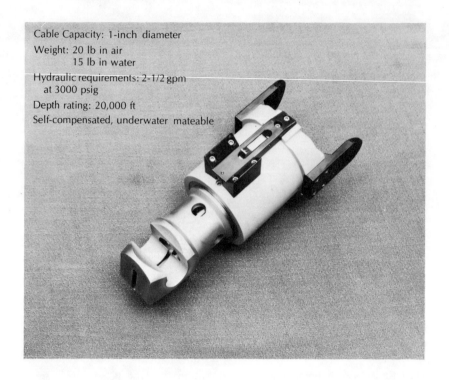

Cable Capacity: 1-inch diameter
Weight: 20 lb in air
        15 lb in water
Hydraulic requirements: 2-1/2 gpm
        at 3000 psig
Depth rating: 20,000 ft
Self-compensated, underwater mateable

FIGURE 2-16   Manipulator-operated cable cutter.

force to sever the cable or bolt instantly. Usually their main parts consist of a squib or primer, and a main charge encased in a single chamber. The squib or primer ignites the main propellant charge, which then produces gas in the required quantity and temperature. The gas produces the useful work (pushing a piston for a cable cutter). Velocity-powered tools are fired either manually (typically using spring-loaded firing pins) or electrically (typically using a heated or exploding bridge-wire embedded in the ignition powder). Many companies produce the devices, and the units have such a solid record of high reliability and ruggedness that they are often used to actuate safety devices, such as marker buoys and weight-jettison devices, on manned submersibles. Figure 2-17 shows a typical commercially available explosively actuated cable cutter for underwater use to 20,000-ft (6100-m) depths.

Of the cutting techniques, sawing and drilling are the most demanding from an operator standpoint. Both require precise position control and large forces. These requirements led to such tools as the suction drill press and rotary impact tools discussed earlier in this chapter. Figure 2-18 shows the thrust required for drilling in AISI 1035 steel. Note that for drilling at the

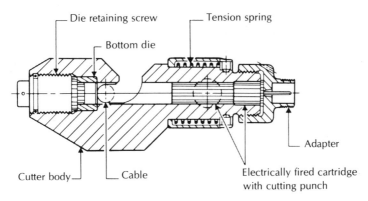

Die retaining screw — Tension spring

Bottom die

Cutter body — Cable

Adapter

Electrically fired cartridge with cutting punch

FIGURE 2-17   Explosively actuated underwater cable cutter. (Courtesy of Mine Safety Appliances Co., Pittsburgh, Pennsylvania.)

recommended feed rate using as small as a ¼-inch-diameter (0.6 cm) drill requires a thrust beyond diver capability. Figure 2-19 shows typical torque values for tapping threads, and Figure 2-20 shows typical torque values for drilling holes.

Figure 2-21 shows a diver-operated linear milling machine. This machine is held in place by suction and can machine a ¾-inch-wide (1.9 cm) by 24-inch-long (61 cm) slot in metal plate up to 2 inches (5 cm) thick. The milling tool is designed to cut large holes in the side of a ship by cutting a series of connecting slots, and is especially useful where explosives are too dangerous and abrasive cutting requires too much time and power.

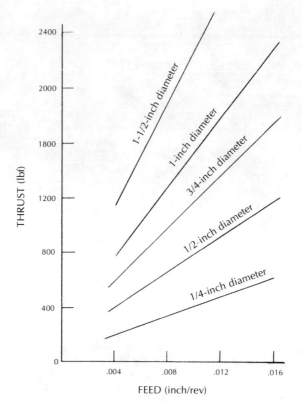

FIGURE 2-18   Thrust required to achieve a given feed for varying drill sizes in AISI 1035 steel (R_c = 22). (Data from Wilson and Harvey, 1959.)

Mechanical Cleaning Tools

Mechanical cleaning tools include such tools as wire brushes, chipping hammers, explosive grit blasters, ultrasonic cleaning tools, and water jets. These tools are used primarily for removing marine growth, corrosion, and scale in preparation for welding or painting or to improve the performance of vessels. As with abrasive saws, wire brushes absorb a large amount of power because of windage losses. Typical windage loss data for several small wire brushes are included in Figure 2-13. Figure 2-22 shows a typical hydraulic-powered, diver-operated wire brush.

Although wire brushing is effective at removing marine growth, it is time consuming and requires the continuous application of high forces. Special systems, such as the SCAMP[R] hull cleaning system shown in Figure 2-23, have been developed for cleaning ship hulls. Contact with the hull is maintained by a pressure differential generated by a centrally located,

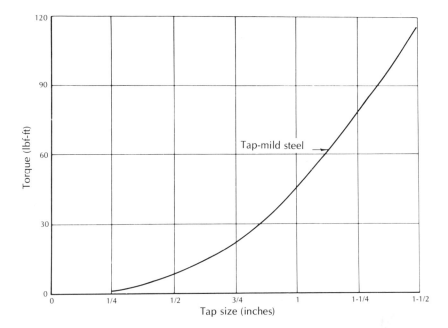

FIGURE 2-19   Typical thread tapping torque (mild steel, coarse threads, 75 percent thread depth, new taps).

hydraulically driven impeller mounted in the machine. The clamping force causes deflection of the three wire brushes (also hydraulically driven) in such a way as to effectively remove fouling by a scything action. This system also has powered wheels for moving along the surface. Other hull cleaning systems have also been designed that typically use suction forces generated by the brush rotation to pull them against the surface to be cleaned. To date, hull cleaners of this type are most effective on substantially flat surfaces, such as those found on super-tankers and other large vessels.

Explosive blasts and ultrasonics have been used with limited success for cleaning surfaces underwater. They require much more energy input than mechanical cleaning and are potentially hazardous to the surface being cleaned or to the operator when used with sufficient power to effectively remove marine material.

Relatively low-pressure water jets (less than 5 bar) are used extensively for removing sediment and trenching. High-pressure water jets (60 bar and higher) have been experimented with for removing marine growth. To date, however, they have not proved very effective because their energy is quickly attenuated by the water and much more energy is required to perform a task than is required by mechanical means.

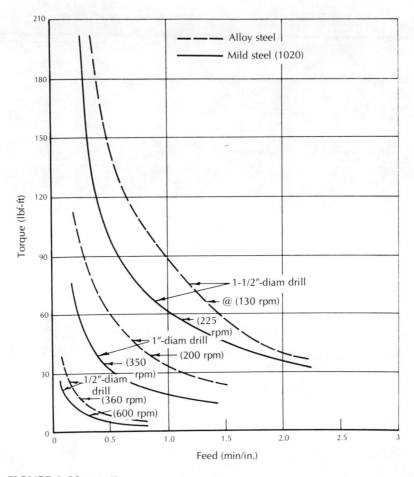

FIGURE 2-20   Drill torque requirements.

Welding

Underwater welding has been used for many years in salvage, repair, and construction. When land welding techniques are used in open water, the process is called "wet" welding. When a pressurized chamber is used to provide a dry environment around either the weld zone or the entire work area, the process is called "dry" welding (Mishler and Randall 1969). Dry welding techniques were first used in mid-1960. They include (1) dry hyperbaric welding done in an open-bottomed chamber that encloses the weld area and one or more welders, (2) minihabitat welding, in which a small chamber is designed to enclose only the weld area and the upper part of the welder/diver's body, and (3) portable dry-box welding, in which a

FIGURE 2-21 Diver-operated underwater milling machine.

small transparent box is sealed against the weld area and the water is displaced by gas from the welding wire feed gun (Grubbs 1977).

Wet Welding. Most welding in underwater salvage and emergency repair is still done wet with the conventional manual shielded metal-arc process (commonly known as stick electrode welding), in which an electric arc is maintained between the work and a 12 to 15-inch-long flux-coated electrode (Figure 2-24). The arc burns in a cavity formed inside the flux covering, which is designed to burn slower than the metal rod of the electrode. Some of the chemical compounds in the electrode coating are vaporized by the arc, and the gases shield the arc from surrounding water and help protect it. The diver exerts a downward pressure on the electrode to keep the flux chipping and burning away to provide a constant arc length (Masubuchi and Tsai 1977). The joint usually is made by laying weld beads in a V-shaped groove formed by lapping or butting the two work pieces to be joined so that the welder-diver can follow the groove

FIGURE 2-22 Diver-operated, hydraulic-powered wire brush. (Manufactured by Underwater Tools & Equipment Co., Orange, California.)

FIGURE 2-23 SCAMP hull cleaning system. (Courtesy of Butterworth Systems Inc.)

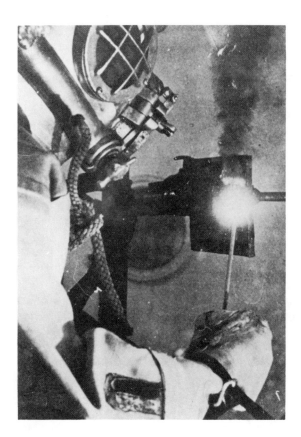

FIGURE 2-24 Conventional wet welding.

with the electrode as welding progresses. This groove is important in limited visibility conditions.

The welder-diver works with an electrode holder that is specially insulated from the water to protect him from electric shock; likewise, all electrical connections of the equipment are insulated. The electrodes are specially formulated for use underwater and are waterproofed to prevent the coatings from disintegrating when immersed in water.

There are numerous advantages to wet welding. The welder-diver can work on portions of structures that, because of complexity of design or location, are difficult to weld by other methods. Repairs can be performed faster and at less cost than by dry welding since it is unnecessary to construct and install enclosures around areas to be welded. Electrode holders designed specifically for underwater welding are available commercially. Readily available standard welding machines and equipment can be used from the surface, allowing wet welding to be easily mobilized at remote job sites.

Myers, Holm, and McAllister (1969) recommend 300-A dc generators for depths to 200 ft (61 m) and 350 to 400-A dc generators for greater depths. Emerson, Angel, and Cox (1967) reported using a 600-A dc generator for welding at depths of 600 ft (182 m). It is generally agreed that welding underwater requires about 25 percent more power than welding on land. Typical current settings are 170 to 210 A for 5/32-inch-diameter (4.0 mm) electrodes and 220 to 260 A for 3/16-inch-diameter (4.8 mm) electrodes when welding in a horizontal or vertical orientation. The voltage drop due to the resistance of the long lengths of cable must also be considered. The minimum recommended size of welding cable is 2/0 for use in Naval service (NAVSHIPS 1969). At 300 A, 2/0 cable has a voltage drop of about 2.7 V per 100 ft (30 m) of cable. The power supply output must be increased to compensate for this increased voltage drop, which increases the open circuit voltage.

Great skill is required to wet weld, and even in the hands of the most skillful welder-diver, wet welding is slow. When changing an electrode, the welder must signal the surface to break the circuit, replace the electrode, position the electrode for welding, and signal the surface to close the circuit. Fillet welding a 6 × 6-inch lifting pad may take an hour, compared with about 15 minutes on land. Since bottom time is expensive, costs can mount rapidly.

Unless carefully performed by skilled divers, wet welds are often of questionable quality, for water acts as a heat sink, reducing heat penetration and causing lack-of-fusion defects. Both tensile strength and ductility have been found to be drastically reduced compared with similar joints in air (Masubuchi and Tsai 1977). The weld and regions next to the weld are likely to crack (underbead cracking) from cooling too rapidly and from the pickup of hydrogen dissociated from water by the arc. It is sometimes possible to lift such welds out of the joint because of underbead cracking. For these reasons, wet welding has been restricted to mild and low-carbon steels. Conventional wet welding techniques have been tested to depths as great as 1200 ft (364 m) (Caudy et al. 1969). Results of the test programs have shown that underwater welds can be made at extended depths by shielded metal-arc welding, although weld quality generally is poor because of weld porosity. Figure 2-25 shows cross sections of wet welds made at a simulated depth of 680 ft (206 m).

Dry Welding.   Dry welding techniques are used most often on submarine pipelines (Grubbs 1977), but also are used for certain external ship repairs (Uhler 1978). The major advantage of dry welding is that it produces high-quality joints as long as proper procedures are used. Dry welds are better than wet welds because cooling rates are slower and hydrogen pickup is minimized. This means that high-strength steels can be

A. Straight Polarity

B. Reverse Polarity

FIGURE 2-25 Cross sections of underwater arc welds made at a simulated depth of 680 ft (206 m).

welded with less danger of weld and underbead cracking. When large chambers are used, the welder can work more efficiently under the improved conditions, which include better visibility.

Hyperbaric chambers for dry welding are complex, costly, cumbersome, limited in work space, and usually require a large barge crane for handling. Minihabitats are less complex and easier to handle, but require that the diver remain in a partly submerged state and in very confined quarters. The portable dry box does not require lifting equipment, but visibility is usually limited by smoke and steam confined in the area of the box.

In addition to the use of stick electrodes, dry welding can be done with either of two other conventional land techniques—the gas-metal-arc (GMA) and gas-tungsten-arc (GTA) processes. Both produce high-quality welds, although they require more elaborate equipment than does the stick electrode method. Stick electrodes, however, may be unsuitable for use in certain manned chambers since the smoke and fumes from the electrode coatings can quickly become intolerable.

In the GMA process, a small-diameter, consumable, bare-wire electrode is fed continuously through the welding torch as fast as the electrode is melted by the arc. The length of the arc between the electrode and the work remains relatively constant. The end of the electrode, the arc, and the molten weld metal are shielded from the atmosphere by argon, helium, carbon dioxide, or a mixture of these gases in order to achieve arc stability and improved weld-metal quality. The gas passes through the welding torch and out of a nozzle that surrounds the electrode. GMA equipment includes a power source, a welding gun, a mechanism for feeding the electrode wire from a spool, and a set of controls. In dry welding, the chamber houses all the GMA equipment except the power supply, which is located on the surface.

GMA is the fastest arc-welding process available for dry welding under-water. On land, a welder can deposit 15 to 20 lb (6.75 to 9 kg) weld metal per hour with manual GMA (compared with 2 to 6 lb (.9 to 2.7 kg) per hour with the stick electrode method). In an underwater chamber, the deposition rate would be about the same. However, the GMA process is difficult to use at diving depths. As the pressure increases with working depth, the arc becomes more intense and melts the filler wire faster; the molten weld pool becomes larger and difficult to control. The excess of molten metal can lead to such weld defects as overlap and improper fusion. Also, with increasing pressure, the shielding gas becomes denser and flow rates up to 10 times the surface rate may be required.

In GTA welding, as in GMA welding, a shielding gas protects the arc, the electrode, and the molten weld metal. The electrode is a tungsten rod instead of a wire with a relatively low melting point, and the arc does not melt the electrode but instead melts the edges of the metal pieces being joined. Filler metal in the form of bare wire is fed into the weld pool as needed. Shielding gas flows through the torch as in GMA welding.

GTA is the only proven way of making pipe welds underwater even though it is slower than GMA. This disadvantage is outweighed by the higher quality of the GTA welds. Also, there are fewer difficulties with GTA welding at diving depths (high pressures).

Experimental Techniques.   Other techniques used for underwater welding include a technique called firecracker welding (Caudy et al. 1979), and explosive welding. Firecracker welding is a version of the shielded metal-arc welding process. Standard flux-covered electrodes are used by placing them in a groove as shown in Figure 2-26, starting the arc, and allowing it to travel unattended along the joint. A typical resulting weld is shown in Figure 2-27. The electrode is held in the joint by a shaped metal block, magnets, or tape. A diver is needed only to set the electrode. Actual welding is accomplished without diver involvement. Important features that differentiate firecracker welding from conventional welding are:

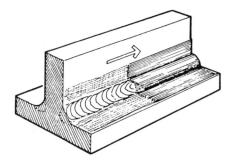

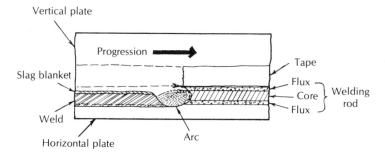

FIGURE 2-26   Schematic of firecracker welding.

- No electrode manipulation is possible; thus, the weld size is determined by the electrode type and diameter.
- Welding speed is fixed by the only independent electrical variable available—current.
- Welds can be effectively made in areas having limited access for a welding operator.
- The electrode length determines the length of weld possible.
- Greater safety is possible where hazardous environments are concerned (such as welding on sunken tankers with unknown cargo) because the diver can leave the area while the arc is running.
- Minimum welding experience is required of the diver to consistently make useful welds.
- Preassembly of attachments to be welded minimizes the need for high visibility before welding.

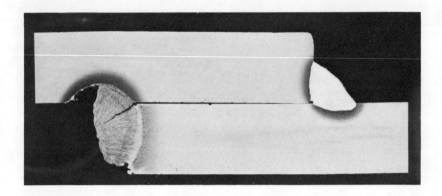

FIGURE 2-27   Cross section of underwater firecracker weld.

Explosive welding techniques have been demonstrated to make sound welds at ambient pressures equivalent to seawater depths of 20,000 ft (6100 m). These welding techniques are especially applicable in making attachments to thick plates. An explosively welded padeye designed for diver use (see Figure 2-28) has two wings that are each covered by a high explosive and two lifting eyes that provide for attachment of a bolt or a cable. The two main charges of explosives on each wing are simultaneously detonated by the use of a cap and lengths of sheet explosives. When the explosives are detonated, the wings are forced against the surface of the object at extremely high controlled velocities. The resulting impact metallurgically bonds the wings of the padeye to the surface of the object with a high-strength weld (see Figure 2-29). The padeye, explosives, and detonating cap are contained in a housing that maintains the alignment of the components and provides a waterproof, gas-filled cover when placed on the surface of the underwater object. The housing has a silicon rubber gasket at the mating surface of the object. The surface of the object must be dry and free of debris and rust on the area to be welded. The unit is held in position with two permanent magnets on either side of the housing. The explosive padeye shown in Figure 2-28 weighs 15 lb (6.75 kg) in water, 20 lb (9 kg) in air, and when correctly bonded, has a lifting capacity of 5,000 lbf (22,250 N).

Thermal Cutting

At one time or another, probably all of the known thermal cutting processes (Table 2-3) have been used for underwater cutting. During the period from before World War I to around the end of World War II (1945),

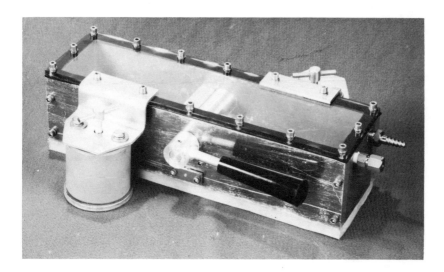

FIGURE 2-28   Explosively bonded padeye for diver use.

oxy-acetylene, oxy-hydrogen, and oxygen-arc cutting were used extensively, particularly in ship salvage operations. Since that time, oxygen-arc
cutting has become more popular and is today the most widely used
underwater cutting process. New processes and materials also have been
used, either experimentally or for actual underwater cutting operations.
The use of the oxy-acetylene and oxy-hydrogen processes has declined
such that today they are only used in special applications.

The applications for underwater cutting and welding are many and
varied, and include construction, repair, and salvage operations. Selection

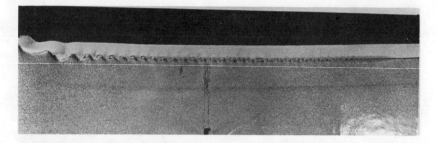

FIGURE 2-29   Cross section of explosively bonded padeye weld.

TABLE 2-3   Thermal processes used for underwater cutting.

Oxy-Fuel Gas Cutting Processes
Oxy-acetylene
Oxy-gasoline
Oxy-natural gas
Oxy-naptha
Oxygen-MAPP[a] gas
Electric Cutting Processes
Air-carbon arc
Bare-metal arc
Carbon arc
Gas-metal arc
Metal arc
Oxygen arc
Plasma arc
Shielded-metal arc
Other Cutting Processes
Liquid oxidizer-liquid fuel (chlorine trifluoride-hydrazine)[b]
Oxygen lance
Pyrotechnic torch

a.   Trade designation of Dow Chemical Company.

b.   Experimental use only.

of the actual process used depends on the depth and nature of the work and on the equipment and fuel or power availability. Advantages of some of the thermal cutting processes are shown in Table 2-4. Gas cutting processes are sometimes specified when there is a possibility of damage from electrolysis if electric cutting were used. Pyrotechnics have been developed for special deep-cutting applications. Explosive cutting (discussed in the following section of this chapter) has been included in Table 2-4 for completeness.

TABLE 2-4   Advantages of various cutting processes. (Adapted from *Underwater Cutting and Welding Manual,* U.S. Naval Ship System Command, 1969.)

Oxygen-Arc Process, Tubular Steel Cutting Electrodes

- Preheating is not required
- Flame adjustments are unnecessary
- Applicable to all metal thicknesses
- Overlapped plates can be cut
- Holidays (skips) can be cut
- Only one gas (oxygen) is needed
- Torches are lightweight
- Less training and skill are required
- Higher cutting rates on thin metal

Oxygen-Arc Process, Ceramic Cutting Electrodes

- Low burnoff rate, long life
- Short length provides easier access in confined spaces
- Light weight improves transportability

Shielded Metal-Arc Process

- Preheating is not required
- Cuts ferrous and nonferrous metals
- Fuel gases and oxygen are not required
- Standard electrode holders can be used in an emergency if properly adapted

Oxy-Hydrogen Process

- Electricity is not required for cutting
- Nonmetallic materials can be severed
- Insulated diving equipment is unnecessary
- Power generators are not required
- There are no ground connections
- Higher cutting rates on thick metal

Oxy-acetylene

- High-flame temperature
- Electricity is not required for cutting
- Insulated diving equipment is unnecessary
- Power generators are not required
- Nonmetallic materials can be severed

Plasma-Arc

- Potentially high cutting rates
- Fuel gases and oxygen are not required
- Cuts ferrous and nonferrous materials

TABLE 2-4   (Continued)

' **Pyrotechnics**

- High cutting rate
- Cuts ferrous and nonferrous metals
- Fuel gases and oxygen are not required

Explosives

- Multiple cuts can be made simultaneously
- High cutting rates
- Fuel gases and oxygen are not required
- Electricity is not required

The underwater oxygen cutting processes are fundamentally the same as those used on land. When cutting with these processes, the steel is preheated to its melting temperature and then a high-velocity stream of high-purity oxygen is directed at the preheated metal to commence cutting. The cutting action depends on chemical reactions between iron and oxygen. The heat generated during these reactions melts some of the iron adjacent to the cut. This molten iron is blown away by the oxygen stream, which also contains some previously formed iron oxide. These new iron layers also become oxidized and liberate heat. Since these oxidation processes are not instantaneous, heat developed at the upper level of the kerf is liberated at the lower level. Consequently, this heat is no longer available at the uppermost level where the oxidation reaction is just beginning. Thus, it is necessary to continually preheat the uppermost level of the material being cut; this is the reason all oxygen cutting torches have continuously burning preheat flames. In oxygen-arc cutting, the arc takes the place of oxy-fuel gas preheat flames.

Before attempting any underwater oxygen cutting on old or encrusted steel, it is necessary first to remove growth, scale, and surface rust. Light growth and scale can be removed with a hand scraper and chipping hammer; heavy growth and hard scale is best removed with power tools. Even after one surface has been cleaned, a heavy rust scale may be present on the other side of the steel plate. Such scale slows the cutting process and consumes additional oxygen and rods. This condition can sometimes be remedied by striking the area to be cut with a heavy sledge hammer to loosen the scale on the opposite side.

Carbon steels can be cut readily by the oxy-hydrogen or oxygen-arc methods. Stainless steel is more difficult to cut by these methods. Steels containing Cr and Ni are not readily oxidized and retard cutting, and graphite in cast iron has the same effect. Brass is not oxidized by the oxygen jet of a conventional torch. For nonferrous metals, such as brass, copper, bronze, or aluminum, other processes, such as shielded metal arc cutting, may be preferable.

Oxy-Fuel Gas Cutting.   The oxy-fuel gas processes are generally used only when there is an absence of generators or other equipment for electric arc cutting. The oxy-fuel gas processes also may be required and specified when electric currents are not desirable because of the possibility of electrolysis, spark formation, or danger from electric shock.

The gases for cutting underwater with the oxy-fuel gas processes are the same as those used in air. However, only one fuel gas, hydrogen, is generally used for underwater cutting. Acetylene has been used, but because of its instability at pressures over about 15 psi (1 bar), it is not used at depths greater than about 25 ft (7.6 m). MAPP gas (stabilized methyl-acetylene propadiene), introduced in 1964, has been used to a limited extent for underwater cutting. Other fuel gases, such as propane and natural gas, also have been used, but generally are not considered effective for underwater cutting. For oxy-fuel gas processes, gas pressures are increased about ½ psi per foot of depth below the surface. Initial gas pressures vary with the kind of torch, kind of gas, and metal thickness.

Oxygen for cutting operations should have a purity of 99.5 percent or higher to maintain cutting efficiency. A 25 percent reduction in cutting speed results from a one percent decrease in oxygen purity. The quality of cut will be reduced and the amount and tenacity of the adhering slag will be increased.

Several oxy-hydrogen and oxy-acetylene underwater cutting torches are available commercially. The torches designed for underwater cutting embody the same design principles as the above water torches except that a shielding cup, skirt, or sleeve is added to provide an air or oxygen bubble to keep water away from the end of the torch tip and to create an artificial atmosphere to ensure proper combustion of the preheat flames. The shielding cup is adjusted so that its outer end projects beyond the tip end, but slightly less than the end point projection of the preheat flame cone. Figure 2-30 shows the gas passages and gas controls in a typical cutting torch. Figure 2-31 shows a typical oxy-fuel gas cutting torch.

Pressure regulators for controlling the flow of gas to the underwater work site must be capable of supplying gas at sufficient pressure to overcome the water pressure at the depth of the work. The torch is usually ignited above water and then lowered to the work site. When ignited above water, the regulators must be adjusted continually while the torch is lowered to the work site. When this process is not practical, gas pressures are preset and the torch is ignited underwater using either an electric spark between the tips of an insulated holder connected to a power supply above the water, a pneumatic-type spark lighter, a chemical capsule, or a gas pilot flame. One type of electrical underwater igniter produces sparks from the making and breaking of electrical contacts. Another type of igniter uses a brass striker plate, and the gas torch nozzle becomes part of the circuit for torch

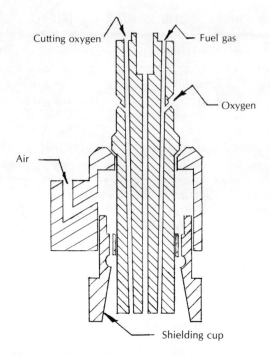

FIGURE 2-30 Typical underwater gas cutting torch tip gas passages and controls.

ignition. The positive lead from a battery is connected to a clip screw on the torch and the negative lead to the striker plate. The battery is located above water and switched into the circuit when called for by the diver-welder. After the current is switched on, the operator obtains a spark by causing a "short" circuit between the nozzle and the striker plate. Powders such as ferrocerium calcium phosphide or sodium metal that ignite spontaneously upon contact with water also have been used (Rodman 1944).

Oxygen-Arc Cutting. Oxygen-arc cutting is similar to oxy-fuel gas cutting except that preheating is accomplished with an electric arc instead of with a flame. The arc is established between a hollow tubular electrode and the metal being cut. The cutting oxygen jet is delivered through the electrode bore to furnish additional heat (from the chemical reaction of oxidation) and to erode the molten metal away by the jetting action of the high-speed oxygen stream. Cutting is performed directly in the water, and no air shield is used.

Steel tubular electrodes, ceramic tubular electrodes, and carbon, graphite, or carbon-graphite electrodes are all used for oxygen-arc cutting. The steel tubular electrode was developed primarily for use in underwater

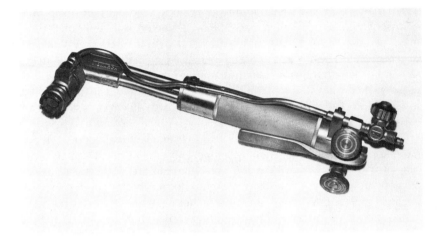

FIGURE 2-31   Typical underwater oxy-fuel gas cutting torch.

cutting and is the most widely used in both commercial and naval service. The major shortcomings of steel tubular electrodes are their short life and their narrow kerf; the narrow kerf interferes with inspection by the diver-welder for incomplete cuts. Ceramic tubular electrodes overcome these disadvantages, but are brittle and expensive. Carbon-graphite type electrodes are also brittle.

Steel tubular oxygen-arc cutting electrodes for underwater cutting consist essentially of a hollow steel tube with a waterproofed outer flux covering. The core of oxygen-arc cutting electrodes is a 14-inch-long (35.6 cm), $^5/_{16}$-inch-outside-diameter (0.79 cm) steel tube having a 0.112-inch-diameter (0.28 cm) bore. Each of these electrodes has a lift of about one minute.

The flux covering is applied only to the outer surface of the electrode, and no flux is contained in the bore. As with stick electrodes used for welding, these coverings aid in starting the arc and in maintaining arc stability, and serve as an electrical insulator that prevents arcing from the side of the electrode when work is done in confined spaces. The coverings are consumed at a slower rate than the core in order to form and maintain a protective sleeve around the arc. One-eighth inch (0.3 cm) of the flux covering is removed from the electrode end to prevent interference with arc starting and about 1½ inches (3.8 cm) are removed from the electrode holder grip area to furnish a bare metal contact area. The flux covering is waterproofed with paint-like materials or tape wrappings to protect it from deterioration in the water. Commercially made underwater electrodes are waterproofed with varnish- or shellac-type materials.

Ceramic tubular electrodes are used for underwater cutting in much the same manner as are steel tubular electrodes. The ceramic electrodes consist of hollow rods of high grade, highly refractory stable silicon carbide or other ceramic materials that are coated with a steel spray coat and waterproofed. The electrodes are ½ inch (1.3 cm) in diameter by 8 inches (20 cm) in length, have a ⅛-inch-diameter (.3 cm) bore, and are coated with $1/_{32}$-inch-thick (0.8 mm) mild steel by metal spraying an arc wrapped in a waterproofed insulating sleeve. One end of the electrode's steel sheath is bare to contact the electrode holder.

The core of a ceramic tubular electrode is an electrical conductor, and has a substantially higher melting temperature than steel. The stable carbides (or oxides) from which the core is made are not affected by the oxygen stream. The electrode is more maneuverable in confined spaces because of its shorter length and longer life; each of these electrodes will last for about 10 minutes (about ten times longer than will a steel tubular electrode when cutting thin or medium thickness steel plate).

Underwater oxygen-arc cutting is especially effective for cutting steel of thicknesses ranging from sheet gages to about 3 inches (7.6 cm). When cutting oxidation-resistant materials, such as cast iron and nonferrous metals, the operator is required to constantly manipulate the oxygen stream to mechanically blow metal out of the kerf, and to constantly manipulate the electrode in and out of the kerf to push out the molten metal that is not removed by the oxygen stream.

Shielded Metal Arc Cutting. Shielded metal arc cutting can be done with practically any kind of properly waterproofed, covered, mild-steel welding electrode. However, cutting rates with the shielded metal-arc cutting process are very low compared with those of oxygen-arc cuttings. Shielded metal-arc cutting is superior to oxygen-arc for cutting cast iron and nonferrous materials. The technique used for shielded metal-arc cutting is the same as the oxygen-arc technique for cutting cast iron and nonferrous metals. Metal is removed by the arc melting the material in the vicinity of the arc followed by a short-stroke sawing motion to push the metal out of the kerf.

When the electrode has been consumed to the point where a change to a new electrode is necessary, the diver-welder signals "current off" to his tender. The electrode is maintained in cutting position until the tender switches the current off with the knife switch and informs the diver. The diver then proceeds with terminating the work or with changing the electrode.

Experimental Techniques. Plasma-arc cutting has been used successfully for limited applications for underwater cutting (Wootke 1960). Plasma-arc cutting involves a constricted arc of extremely high temperature and velocity between an electrode and the piece to be cut. The arc is constricted by passing it through a nozzle with a small-diameter orifice; it is thereby localized so that its intense heat melts the metal. The gas, which is preheated by the arc, expands and is accelerated as it is forced through the constricting orifice. The metal that is melted is then continuously removed by the jet-like action of the gas stream to form a kerf. The combined heat and force of the arc stream produce a high-quality, sawlike cut. Where inert gases are used, the cutting process depends solely upon thermal action. When such materials as mild steel and cast iron are being cut, increased cutting speeds can be achieved by using oxygen-bearing cutting gases. In this case, the chemical energy of combination is added to the arc heat to permit higher speeds. The plasma-arc cutting process can be used to cut any metal.

Electron-beam equipment has been used experimentally in preliminary underwater cutting and welding experiments. Schumacher (1967) reports that underwater electron-beam cutting of rock has been demonstrated. The electron beam produced a melt cut about 2 inches deep that, when combined with thermal stresses, caused cracking of the rock. The work was performed in only a few inches of water with the electron-gun muzzle submerged only a few inches. The gun-to-work distance was ¼ to ½ inch—about the same as that for electron-beam welding in the open atmosphere.

A version of the oxygen lance known as a burning bar has been used for underwater cutting (NAVSHIPS 1969). The burning bar consists of iron pipe filled with aluminum and magnesium wires. One end of the bar is gripped in a special holder that is connected to an oxygen supply. In operation, the free end of the bar is heated until red with an oxy-acetylene or other suitable flame. After the end of the bar is heated, a stream of oxygen is forced through the bar, igniting the hot end. The burning end of the bar is then manipulated in the zone to be cut. The normal life of a 10-ft-long (3 m) burning bar is about 5 minutes. The burning bar has been used extensively above water for cutting a variety of materials, including concrete, slag, brick, steel, cast iron, aluminum, and bronze. However, accidents due to the explosion of gases trapped in the cutting cavity have occurred when burning bars have been used underwater.

Pyrotechnic torches can also be used for the cutting or perforation of heavy steel plate, chain, cable, or pipe (Rozner and Helms 1976). Pyrotechnic torches use an exothermic powder mixture of nickel, aluminum, iron oxide, and a flurocarbon. The material is pelletized and incorporated into specially designed cylindrical casings that contain a nozzle and an initiation system (Figure 2-32). The initiation system consists of an electrically actuated explosive squib (similar to those in explosively actuated cable cutters discussed earlier under mechanical cutters). The heat generated by the exploding squib ignites the exothermic mixture; the resultant molten metals and oxides are ejected at high velocity through the

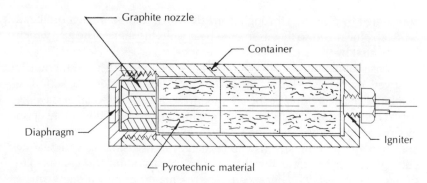

FIGURE 2-32   Cross section of pyrotechnic cutting torch.

nozzle and impinge on the object to be cut. The impact of the liquid jet against the object produces rapid cratering and perforation of the object. The cutting ability decreases with depth, but successful cuts have been made in excess of 3000 ft (900 m). Figure 2-33 shows a 1⅝-inch-diameter (4.1 cm) wire rope that was cut in shallow water using a pyrotechnic cutter.

Explosive Cutting.   Explosives have been used extensively underwater. Explosive cutting is particularly useful when there is limited time available to perform a task or when there is danger to the diver or submersible from the release of material or from the shifting of structures

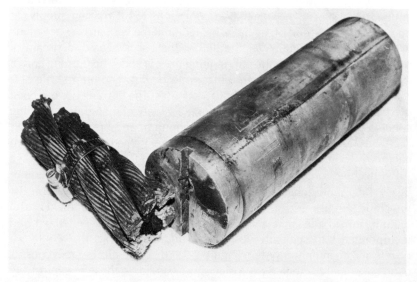

FIGURE 2-33   1-⅝-inch-diameter (4.1 cm) wire rope cut with pyrotechnic torch.

caused by the cutting. Most of the early uses of explosive cutting were for demolition work in which an obstacle was destroyed or removed by blowing it to pieces. Cleaning submerged rocks, performing underwater ditching, removing tree stumps, and demolishing coffer dams were accomplished in this manner.

Previously, controlled underwater cutting was accomplished by using strings of explosives to destroy an object within a localized area. Localized blasting is now accomplished by means of a shaped charge. The shaped charge contains a metal liner that is given a velocity by the explosive. As the shock front travels through the explosive charge, it attacks the liner at a high pressure, which sends pressure shock waves through the liner wall, resulting in failure of the metal of the opposite surface. The liner impacts the target with such extreme pressure that it forces the target material to flow radially from the point of impact. This action is similar to that occurring when a high-velocity stream of water is directed at a relatively soft soil formation. Small particles of the liner are thrown free at velocities approaching 30,000 ft/s (9000 m/s). This shaped charge configuration can be formed in a circle to cut inwardly or outwardly or can be formed in almost any configuration to achieve a desired cutting action of any shape. The charge can be detonated by attaching detonating cord or through the use of a blasting cap. Shape charges can be used underwater for virtually any cutting application.

Figure 2-34 shows an explosive hole punch designed to cut a 4-inch-diameter (10.2 cm) hole in 2-inch-thick (5.1 cm) steel plate at depths of 1000 ft (305 m) of seawater. The tool is designed to be installed by a diver, held in place with magnets, and remotely actuated. Figure 2-35 shows a cross section of the explosive hole punch. The V-shaped metal liner directs the cutting power in a ring. In Goodfellow (1977), several photographs are provided of shaped charges used for cutting pipe, holes in pipe, structural beams, cables, and chain, and Penzias (1973) includes a detailed discussion of the cutting action. With proper design, explosives can perform useful work at all depths of the ocean.

Attachments

The ability to make simple, reliable attachments to work objects underwater is a major problem in many underwater operations. Underwater salvage and small object recovery operations require firm, reliable attachments to withstand dynamic loads during breakout from the seafloor, winching to the surface, hoisting aboard ship, and towing to shallow water. Similarly, simple, reliable attachment methods are needed for making temporary repairs to ship hulls and for the lifting and movement of such items as pipe and valves in pipeline and subsea completion systems. Many

FIGURE 2-34   Explosive hole punch.

different methods and schemes of attachment have been proposed and carried to various stages of development. No one method has proven to be adequate for all requirements. Table 2-5 lists a number of attachment methods presently used underwater along with descriptions of typical applications for each method.

Standard rigging techniques, including the manual installation of slings, shackles, choker cables, and various harnesses, are often used by divers for making attachments. However, unless rigging devices are specially designed for remote use, their use with most manipulators is difficult or impossible. Figure 2-36 shows an anchor chain being rigged for recovery by the U.S. Navy's Remote Unmanned Work System vehicle using a special line-handling technique that involves inserting a small line and passing increasingly larger lines through the chain.

For remote attachment, probably the most straightforward method of attachment is the use of a claw or grabber sized to fit the object. Such devices are used extensively for the recovery of ordnance, especially torpedoes (Smith 1968). They have also been used for the recovery of large-diameter communications cable (NAVSEA 1971), and reportedly for the recovery of large portions of submarines (Burleson 1977). Figure 2-37 shows a mechanical claw used with a tethered vehicle for the successful

TABLE 2-5 Typical underwater attachment methods.

Attachment Method	Typical Application	Remarks
Mechanical or hydraulic claw	Ordnance and small object recovery, communication cable recovery	Extensively used in torpedo recovery. Has been used for large objects.
Grapnel	Hooking lines, parachutes, nets, soft materials	
Velocity-powered devices	Attachment of lifting pad-eyes, salvage hose fittings, temporary patches	Propellant charge must be adjusted for stud size and material thickness
Nets	Recovery of irregularly shaped objects and miscellaneous debris	
Snares	Recovery of ordnance or irregularly shaped objects	Simple loop or lasso
Toggle bar	Attachment through structural openings	Easily fabricated at the salvage site. Used for Alvin recovery.
Self-tapping fasteners	Attachment of lifting pad-eyes and temporary patches	
Welding	Attachment of lifting pad-eyes and patches	
Slings	Generally used on large objects	Must have access to circumference or jetting capability
Magnets	Temporary attachment to iron or steel objects	Generally require a clean surface
Blind fasteners	Attachment of padeyes, lugs or special fixtures	Pop-rivet type requires fairly accurate hole
Vacuum attachments	Temporary attachment to objects having flat, smooth surfaces	Holding force diminishes as it approaches the surface
Snap hooks	Attachment of line to padeyes, bales, anchors	
Spring-loaded shackle	Attachment of lines to large padeyes	Used with remote control vehicles
Adhesives	Small object recovery and temporary repairs	Clean, relatively smooth surfaces required
Standard rigging	Anchor chains, structural members, irregularly shaped objects	Difficult to do with manipulators

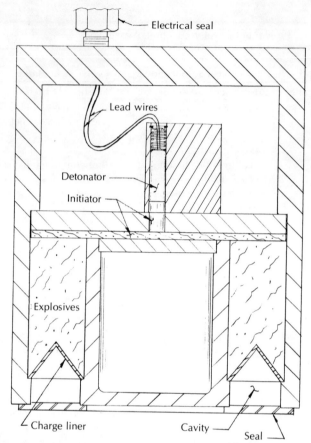

FIGURE 2-35 Cross section of explosive hole punch.

recovery of several 7000-lb (3175-kg) lengths of communications cable from 3000-ft (1000-m) depths. The device is spring loaded to the closed position, is mechanically interlocked to stay closed once actuated, and has a linkage that causes the jaws to clamp the wire more tightly as the load lifted increases.

Velocity-power-driven studs depend upon the energy from an explosive charge to propel a stud into a plate or structural members. The stud can then be used for bolting on a plate, flange, or lifting padeye. Figure 2-38 shows various types of commercially available studs. Velocity-power-driven stud guns have been used extensively by divers (see Figure 2-39) and to some extent by submersibles. One limitation is that the propellant charge must be adjusted to the stud size and material thickness. Another limitation is that the stud spalls off a shower of sparks when driven into a gas-filled tank, which can be hazardous with unknown cargoes.

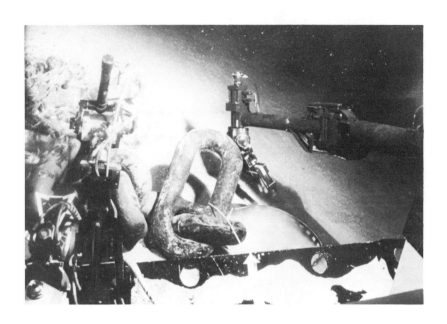

FIGURE 2-36 Anchor chain recovery by U.S. Navy's Remote Unmanned Work System. (Courtesy of Naval Ocean Systems Center, Hawaii Laboratory.)

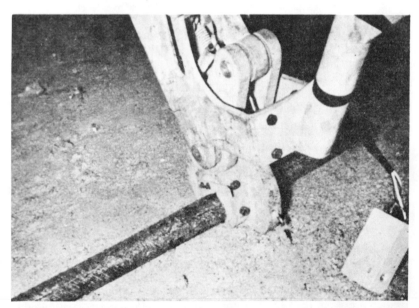

FIGURE 2-37 Underwater cable grabber used by the U.S. Navy's CURV II vehicle to recover communications cable. (Courtesy of Naval Sea Systems Command, U.S. Navy.)

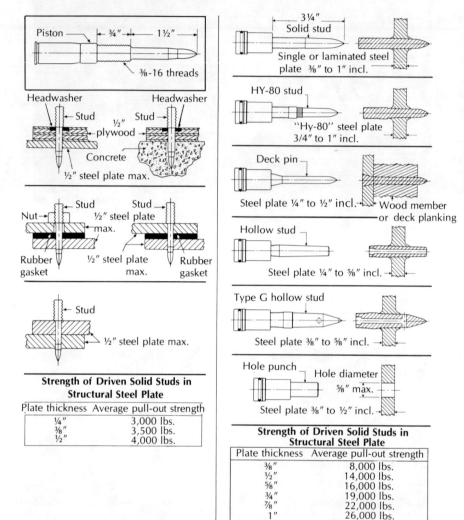

FIGURE 2-38 Velocity-powered tool projectiles. (Courtesy of Mine Safety Appliances Co., Pittsburgh, Pennsylvania.)

Toggle attachments consist of a structural link to which an attachment cable has been fastened, and a pivoting toggle bar, which is pinned to the link. Toggles are operated by inserting a device in a folded configuration through a hole in the object. After insertion, the toggle bar is allowed to rotate so that it cannot be withdrawn. If the material bordering the hole in which the device has been inserted is strong enough, the object can be lifted with a toggle. A toggle was used to salvage the Alvin submersible

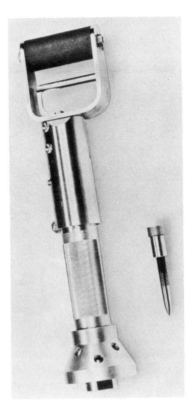

FIGURE 2-39   Velocity-powered underwater stud driver for diver use. (Courtesy of Mine Safety Appliances Co., Pittsburgh, Pennsylvania.)

when it was dropped in 5000 ft (1520 m) of water in 1969 (NAVSHIPS 1979).

Conventional welding attachments have been limited to a few hundred feet, although explosive welding techniques have been used experimentally to deeper depths. Both techniques were covered earlier in this chapter.

Due to the variations in the holding force that can be obtained with a given magnet under different circumstances and to their limitation to only magnetic materials, magnets are not a reliable type of attachment device. They are generally used in applications where tools, padeyes, or vehicles must be temporarily held in place while a work task is being performed.

Vacuum attachments have been used for temporary attachments of many types (see Figures 1-2 and 2-21). Unlike on the surface, where the maximum differential pressure obtainable by evacuating a cavity is equal to the atmospheric pressure, the vacuum obtainable underwater is equal to the absolute ambient pressure at the working depth. Thus, at deep depths, very high lifting forces can be generated over a small area using a vacuum attachment. For recovery-type operations, vacuum devices have not proven practical to date because the holding force diminishes as the object approaches the surface.

Underwater curable adhesives are available that can be applied to a variety of materials and that do not require a knowledge of the material type or thickness as does the use of power-driven studs. Adhesives do not require extensive support equipment or highly trained personnel (such as required for welding) and can be used to spread the load over a large area, which is important for attaching to fragile objects.

Adhesives are normally applied manually; it is important that surfaces be clean prior to the application. When manually applied, the adhesive is spread on mating surfaces or injected between the surfaces to be bonded. A restraining force must be applied to keep the mating surfaces together during the curing cycle. To date, underwater adhesives have been unreliable in bonding strength, especially over large areas. On small areas (a few square inches or centimeters), typical shear strengths of 400 to 1000 psi (2760 to 7000kPa) are obtained, but on larger areas the shear strengths drop drastically. This drop is sometimes attributed to water entrapment within the adhesive preventing complete bonding. Recently, some adhesives have become available that have the capability of expelling the water from within the adhesive joint. However, even for these adhesives, experiments have yielded shear strength values of about 400 psi (2760kPa).

3

UNDERWATER POWER SOURCES

DIVER, pneumatic, hydraulic, electric, and explosive energy are all used to power underwater tools. Because the power output of a diver is limited to a fraction of a horsepower for a few minutes and to relatively low total force outputs, diver-powered tools have been limited to hand tools and to small tools powered by hand- or foot-operated hydraulic pumps. Pneumatic, hydraulic, and electric power have all been used extensively underwater. In addition, explosive power has been used for special-purpose applications.

PNEUMATIC POWER

Air motors, air cylinders, air-powered lift pumps, and air bags all rely on compressed gas for power. Air bags have been used since the early days of diving for lifting sunken objects. Small bags often use a diver's own air, but larger systems usually carry their own compressed gas supply or rely on a gas generator. Air lift systems have also been used many years in dredging systems and are now being used experimentally for deep ocean mining. Air cylinders are used as relatively low-force linear actuators. Air motors, the primary subject of this section, have been used extensively in shallow-water work tools because of their ease of adaptation from industrial uses.

Air motors provide compact, lightweight sources of power. They are not harmed by overloading, rapid reversals, or continuous stalling, can start and stop rapidly, and provide stepless, adjustable control of torque and speed (Hackman and Glasgow 1967). Air motors commonly used for power tools obtain only a small portion of their energy from the controlled expansion of the compressed air. Air is admitted at full reservoir pressure for essentially the whole intake stroke; in this respect, the operation is similar to a hydraulic motor. The cooling effect of the expanding air limits the amount of useful expansion to about 20 percent expansion (Willoughby 1972) because of the danger of freezing entrained moisture within the motor. If air were expanded through an air motor near the ratio of initial compression (7/1 for a 90 psi (620 kPa) line pressure with atmospheric exhaust), an expansion from a 40°F (4°C) initial temperature would end at −154°F (−103°C), which probably would freeze the motor. Motors that are designed to provide an appropriate expansion ratio in surface use generally perform satisfactorily underwater because the submerged exhaust components are warmed by the surrounding water.

Available power in air motors ranges from ⅛ to 25 hp (0.1 to 19 kW), and loaded speeds from 40 to 6,000 rpm with some much higher (Willoughby 1972). Most commercially available pneumatic-powered tools utilize air pressure in the vicinity of 90 psig (7 bar abs). The exhaust air typically is vented directly from the air motor. This venting can be a nuisance to the operator, and thus a short exhaust line often is attached to exhaust the air away from the diver.

Pneumatic power systems may use an open circuit, in which the tool exhausts into the water, or a closed circuit, in which the exhaust returns to the compressor. The open pneumatic circuit has the disadvantage that, as working depth increases, a larger part of the work done by the supply compressor is used in exhausting against the water head. This is shown in Figure 3-1, which includes the isentropic compression from ambient air temperature, the effect of a 100 percent effective after-cooling of the compressed air due to the long hose length underwater, and the portions of the remaining square-card energy that can ideally perform useful work at the tool.

The pressure increase due to the operating depth and the flow pressure drop in the tool supply line characteristically has limited the use of open-circuit pneumatic tools to about 150 ft (45 m) of water. The practical considerations that lead to this limitation include: (a) the control of the air supply pressure must vary over a significant range with working depth; (b) the range of working conditions must compromise the design of the

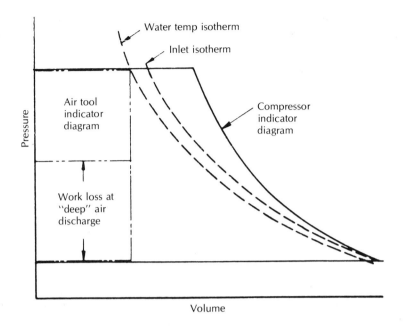

FIGURE 3-1   Typical open cycle air-motor thermodynamics.

compressor; (c) poor energy utilization increases the cost of the air to the tool; and (d) the large air flow requirements at depth necessitate a large compressor capacity. A typical tool operating at 100 psig (690 kPa) and requiring 8.5 ft³ (0.24 m³) of free air per minute at the surface would require 26 ft³ (0.74 m³) of free air per minute at 500 ft (150 m).

Closed-circuit pneumatic tools would not be as energy wasteful at depth if supply line sizes were large. However, a closed-circuit pneumatic tool would be required to withstand the full water pressure or the entire system would have to be operated at elevated pressures. These complexities, in addition to the cumbersome hose required, have prevented the development of closed-circuit pneumatic systems except for the use of small air turbines in scale-model testing.

HYDRAULIC POWER

Hydraulic systems use a liquid as the energy transmission medium. Hydraulic motors and actuators, like pneumatic motors and actuators, have rapid start and stop capabilities, and can provide a wide variation in speed, torque, or force. An advantage of hydraulic motors over pneumatic motors is the elimination of air bubbles that can cloud vision. However, hydraulic circuits often leak small amounts of working fluid, which can be messy on the surface or can cause contamination below.

Closed hydraulic systems, which recirculate the working fluid, and open hydraulic systems, which discharge the working fluid into the sea, are both used. Closed hydraulic circuits are well proven in surface as well as in underwater use. They usually use oil as the working fluid. In addition to providing a medium for power transmission, the oil serves as a lubricant for the internal moving components (motors, cylinders, and rotary actuators) and assists in retarding corrosion in the internal moving parts (especially if there is seawater intrusion).

Most hydraulic-powered diver tools use conventional hydraulic power supplies in which a hydraulic pump is driven by an electric motor or by an internal combustion engine. The hydraulic pump draws the hydraulic oil from a reservoir and supplies the oil to the tool via a long pressure line. A separate return line returns the tool's exhaust to the reservoir. Since hydraulic oil typically has a density of 0.7 to 0.9 times that of water, the pressure differential across seals at normal diver depths is low enough, even when oil in the circuit is not flowing, that conventional surface hydraulic tools can be used with little modification or degradation in performance. However, tools designed specifically for closed circuit use underwater usually incorporate corrosion-resistant materials internally and externally and have improved seals.

When a closed circuit similar to that shown in Figure 3-2 is used to supply tools through long hydraulic hoses, viscous losses can become significant. Figure 3-3 shows typical pressure drops in hydraulic lines for various line sizes and oil viscosities. Viscosity, probably the most important property to be considered in the selection of a hydraulic fluid, expresses the readiness with which a fluid flows. A more viscous fluid (higher viscosity) exhibits more resistance to flow than a less viscous (lower viscosity) fluid. Viscosity is strongly affected by temperature, with oil becoming less viscous as temperature decreases. Pressure also has a minor effect on viscosity. Figures 3-4 and 3-5 show these effects for some representative oils. One important feature of underwater hydraulic systems is that even during tool operation the oil temperature often remains near the temperature of the water. This feature must be considered in selecting the oil.

When closed-circuit hydraulic systems are used for depths beyond about 200 feet (60 m), the hydraulic pump and reservoir are usually located underwater near the tool. The hydraulic pump is usually powered by a battery or a surface-powered electric motor. Such a system eliminates long hydraulic lines, but requires the use of sealed reservoirs that are either pressure compensated so that the oil-filled reservoir pressure is nearly the same as the ambient pressure around the power supply or strong enough

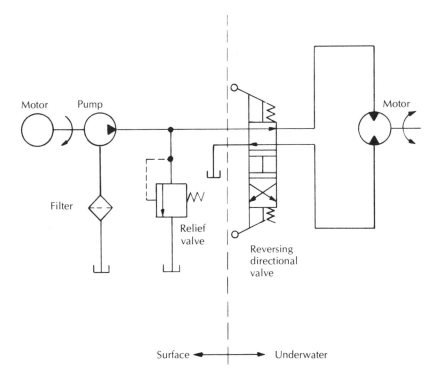

Motor   Pump

Motor

Filter

Relief
valve

Reversing
directional
valve

Surface ◄──────► Underwater

FIGURE 3-2   Typical surface-supplied, closed-circuit hydraulic tool circuit.

that the entire system can withstand the external pressure at depth.

Open hydraulic systems use seawater as the working fluid, which eliminates the need to store a large quantity of fluids only to throw them away at
the exhaust. The use of seawater as the working fluid decreases the seal
requirements and allows elimination of the reservoir and return lines.
However, a suitable filter system is required to remove organic and inor-
ganic materials. Seawater hydraulic systems have been used effectively in
high-flow pumping operations associated with some ocean mining
schemes. In these cases, the components have been relatively high-
volume, low-pressure systems with low speed and minimal precision
requirements.

Open hydraulic systems for use in powering small manipulator- or
diver-operated tools have not been used extensively to date, primarily
because of the corrosiveness, lack of lubrication, and abrasiveness of
seawater on typical hydraulic components. A considerable amount of
work has been done within the U.S. Navy in developing ceramics, refractory alloys, and special coatings that can be used to make conventional
hydraulic components (Black 1976; CEL 1978). To date, the programs

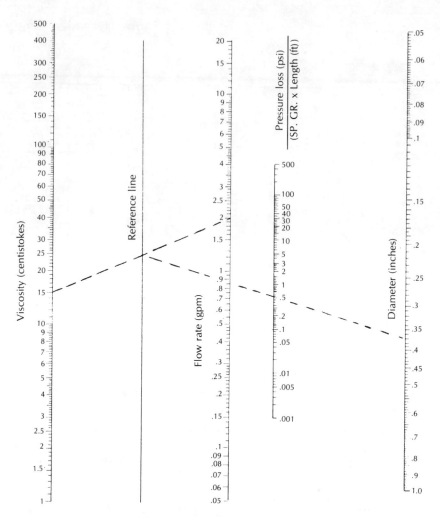

FIGURE 3-3 Pressure drop versus flow rate for various line sizes and oil viscosities. (Example: Flow rate = 2 gpm. Kinematic viscosity = 15 centistokes. Tube diameter = 0.38 inches. Connect flow rate and viscosity. From same point on reference line, connect to bore. Pressure loss readoff = 0.50 psi. This is pressure loss per foot of pipe divided by the specific gravity of the fluid.)

have met with some success (CEL 1980), but successful tools promise to be very expensive. In particular, water-lubricated bearings and improved seals need further development before seawater tools are cost effective.

ELECTRIC POWER

Electric-powered tools are the most widely used portable tools on land. They are reliable, convenient, easy to use, efficient, and well developed.

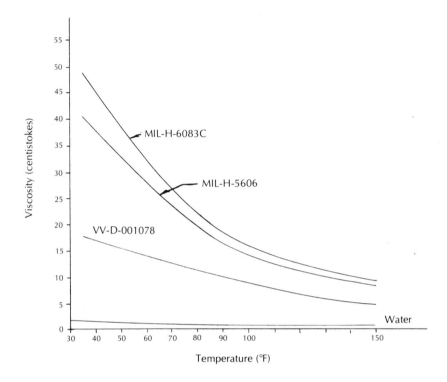

FIGURE 3-4   Viscosity versus temperature for various oils. (Adapted from Mc-Quaid and Brown 1972.)

Although the use of conventional electric motors underwater is limited because of the susceptibility of insulation to moisture and the possible shock hazard, specially designed electric motors may be conveniently used underwater. The important components in the electrical system are the motor and the power source.

When electric motors are used in water, provisions must be made so that no sealed conductors can come into contact with the water. Submersible electric motors are widely used as vehicle-propulsion units and in submersible pumps. They are efficient, convenient, and reliable in underwater use. There are three basic types of submersible electric motors: sealed, pressure equalized, and open.

The sealed motor (see Figure 3-6) uses an ac or dc motor enclosed in a housing and sealed at the output shaft. This arrangement has the advantage of using a standard electric motor. Its disadvantages are that the housing and seal must withstand all of the external pressure. Any seal leakage would be detrimental to the motor.

The pressure-equalized motor (see Figure 3-7) is also enclosed in a housing, but it is filled with a nonconducting fluid. A thin diaphragm

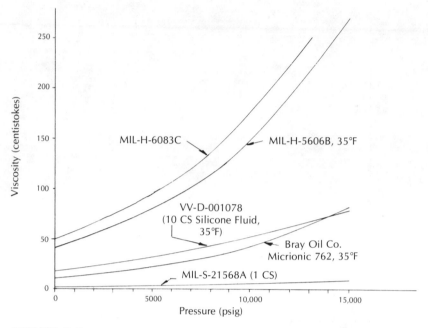

FIGURE 3-5 Viscosity versus pressure for various oils. (Adapted from Mc-Quaid and Brown 1972.)

transmits the external pressure to the fluid. The housing and seal have very little pressure differential across them. All components, including the electrical insulation, must withstand the presence of the fluid, and the viscous drag due to the rotor rotating in oil decreases the overall efficiency. This design is widely used for battery-powered systems that use conventional dc motors with brushes. Such motors must have excellent commutation characteristics or the resultant brush arcing can fill the compensating oil with carbon and cause shorting within the windings.

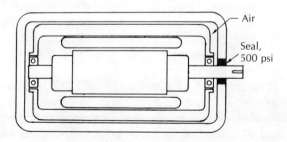

FIGURE 3-6 Sealed motor.

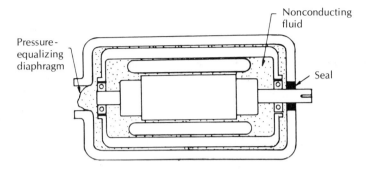

FIGURE 3-7   Pressure-equalized motor.

The open motor (see Figure 3-8) has all components open to water and must, therefore, be corrosion resistant and isolated from the electric circuit. The open motor has the advantages of being smaller, lighter in weight, and lower in cost than other motors. It does not require seals and is not depth sensitive. If a motor is to be open, it must be a brushless motor. The most desirable type of brushless motor is the three-phase induction motor, although single-phase circuits can be used. A single-phase capacitor-start induction motor is suitable for heavy-duty application requiring high stall torque and high efficiency. Field windings must be insulated from the shorting effect of the conducting seawater. This can be accomplished by using insulated wire or by encapsulating the entire coil in a waterproof sealant. A three-phase ac source gives the motor good starting and reversing characteristics without the addition of auxiliary windings.

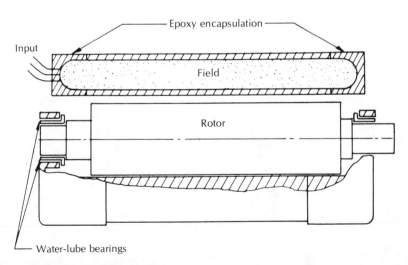

FIGURE 3-8   Open submersible motor.

Electric motors can be powered by batteries, a fuel cell, a cable from the surface, a vehicle, or a habitat. Nuclear-powered thermoelectric generators are also widely used underwater, but only for long-term, low-power applications. Underwater power cables and connectors are well developed and are readily available. The reliability and safety of underwater cables are increased when a grounded shield is used so that, if the outer insulation is damaged, the ground is exposed rather than the power conductor.

Battery-operated motors have the advantage of being completely portable without trailing hoses, lines, or cable. Electric motors can be operated at a low voltage, such as 6 to 12 V, thereby reducing the shock hazard. But most battery-powered systems operate at voltages in the 60 to 120 V range to minimize electric wire size and to allow the use of lightweight motors. However, batteries also present certain disadvantages. During charge and deep discharge, the battery is under stress that can cause rupture. Even the so-called sealed batteries release gases during charging. The danger of rupture and emission of gases requires that batteries be charged in safe areas and that even the sealed batteries not be charged in pressure containers.

Lead acid batteries are the most widely used batteries underwater. Typically they are pressure compensated by filling the void above the battery electrolyte with nonconducting oil. Recently, silver-zinc batteries have also come into wide acceptance for deep submergence use because of their high energy-to-volume and energyy-to-weight ratios. Table 3-1 summarizes weight and energy data for several types of storage batteries.

Fuel cells have also been developed for deep ocean use, and generally offer a weight savings over batteries for systems requiring more than a few hundred kilowatt hours of energy storage. Fuel cells must be sized to the maximum expected peak load, while battery systems can be expected to withstand short overloads.

There is always the danger of electric shock in using electrical equipment. Electric shock can inhibit the respiratory center and likewise can affect the heart by initiating ventricular fibrillation and cardiac arrest (Hackman and Glasgow 1967). It is widely believed that contact with a

Table 3-1 Storage battery characteristics [a]

	Watt-Hour Pound	Watt-Hour (Inch)^3
Lead Acid	8.4	0.7
Silver Cadmium	21	1.7
Silver Zinc	33	2.2
Nickel Zinc	21	1.3

a. Includes an oil compensation system.

power line carrying a high voltage will result in respiratory paralysis, while contact with current of lower voltage, such as 110, 220, or 500 V used in households and industry, can affect the heart. Although the voltage of the source apparently affects the path through the body, it is the resulting current that causes the damage.

Table 3-2 summarizes typical physical effects of current on the body (Hackman and Glasgow 1967; Penzias and Goodman 1973). When a human is subjected to an electric current, most of the body resistance is in the skin. Average hand resistances are 3600 ohm, dry; 1000 ohm, sweating; and 500 ohm, wet (Hackman and Glasgow 1967).

TABLE 3-2   Shock-current intensities and their effects[a].

Current in Milliamperes	Effect
1	Threshold of perception
5–15	Unpleasant stimulation
15–19	Paralysis of muscles through which current flows
25	Possible permanent damage to tissues and blood vessels
70 and higher	May be lethal

a.   Approximate values for 60 Hz current.

The total effect of current on the body depends on time as well as on current (Dalziel 1962). A high current can be withstood if it falls to 50 mA within 50 millisecond. This time is about equal to 3 cycles of 60-cycle current. Therefore, if the current can be cut off in 3 cycles, permanent damage to the operator may be avoided. The power can be cut off in this short time by means of a safety trip circuit, as shown schematically in Figure 3-9(a). This safety trip circuit allows the current to be cut off by the relay that has current passing through its coil when the load becomes unbalanced by a short. Other protection systems (grounding and insulation) are shown in (b) and (c) of Figure 3-9. Since electric power is always potentially dangerous, it is necessary to build underwater tools so that there are always redundant safety precautions.

EXPLOSIVE POWER

Explosives are used as a power source for many underwater tools, including the velocity-powered mechanical cutter, explosive welding, explosive cutting, and explosive attachment tools discussed in Chapter 2. Explosives are generally classified as either (1) "detonating" or "high" explosives or (2) "deflagrating" or "low" explosives (Cook 1958). High explosives are characterized by very high rates of reaction (flame front velocities of 1 to 6

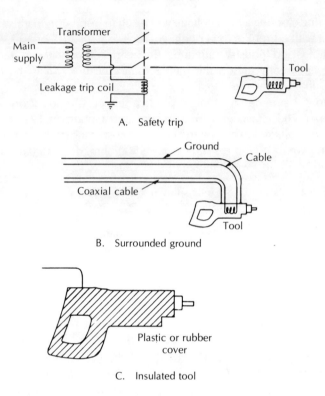

A. Safety trip

B. Surrounded ground

C. Insulated tool

FIGURE 3-9 Electrical protection systems. (Hackman and Glasgow 1967.)

miles/s [1600 to 10,000 m/s]) and high pressures of explosion (50,000 to 4,000,000 psi [0.34 to 27 GPa]). Because of the high rates of explosion, these explosives are used in demolition, blasting, and shaped charges, and are generally not suitable for use as propellants in guns or in velocity-powered tools.

Low explosives burn much slower than high explosives (flame front velocities of ⅓ to 1 mile/s [540 to 1600 m/s]) and develop much lower pressures (up to about 50,000 psi [0.34 GPa]). Low explosives are particularly useful for single actuation devices, such as velocity-powered cable cutters. The energy density of some typical explosive cartridges used as propellants is in the range of 360,000 to 440,000 ft-lbf of energy per lb of explosive (1100 to 1300 J/g) (Batori 1974; U.S. Army Material Command 1963). High explosives often have energy densities in the 980,000 to 2,500,000 ft-lbf/lb (2900 to 7500 J/g) range.

UNDERWATER DESIGN CONSIDERATIONS

IN the design of underwater tools, it is necessary to select materials for fabrication that are compatible with or can be protected from the environment and to utilize design techniques suitable for the depth at which the tool will be used. This chapter discusses good design practices, with emphasis on the areas of material selection, protective coatings, and compensation for the increased pressure at depth.

MATERIAL SELECTION

Materials selected for underwater tools either must have inherent resistance to the corrosive effects of seawater or else steps must be taken to protect them. Most plastics and elastomers have excellent resistance to deterioration by seawater, while metals vary considerably in their resistance to deterioration from the corrosive effects of seawater. However, although plastics or elastomers should be utilized where possible for their desirable properties, they often lack the strength, stiffness, hardness, fabricability, or wear properties needed in a specific design application. Thus, metals are used for the majority of underwater components.

Metals

Steel has long been the principal material for marine applications because of its strength, ease of fabrication, and low cost (Masubuchi 1971). Low-carbon and low-alloy steels are the most widely used steels for ships and structures. However, for underwater tools and manipulators, material costs are less significant than fabrication costs, and carbon steels are used only to a limited extent. Austenitic stainless steels (particularly 304 and 316) are used in lower strength components and aluminum alloys are used extensively in tools where light weight and excellent machinability are important. Where high strength and hardness are required, such as in hammers, shafts, and tool bits, high-carbon, high-alloy tool steels are used with suitable coatings for corrosion protection. In applications where high strength is important but hardness is not so critical, precipitation-hardening stainless steels, such as 17-4, 17-7, and 13-8, and titanium or Inconel 625 or 700 are often used. However, the precipitation-hardening stainless steels must be properly heat treated or stress crack corrosion can occur.

Table 4-1 shows the galvanic series for various metals and alloys in seawater. The galvanic series provides an indication both of the severity with which a metal will be corroded when used unprotected in seawater, and of which metals will accelerate the corrosion of another metal when electrically connected to it in seawater. In general, the more noble a metal, the lower the rate at which it will corrode in seawater. Also, a less noble metal will tend to protect a more noble metal from corrosion when electrically coupled to it. However, there are many exceptions and additional considerations that can alter the relationship.

Corrosion is basically an electrochemical action much like that in an electric dry cell. An electric current flows between metal areas through an electrolyte (seawater) and the metal deteriorates or corrodes where the current leaves the metal and enters the solution. This point is called the anode. The positive ions of metal enter the solution at the anode while the electrons leave the point of corrosion and flow through the metal to the cathode. The cathode is the point where the current returns to the metal or to another metal in electrical contact. A potential difference is necessary for corrosion to occur; it may be caused by two different materials in contact in seawater, or by differences in potential at two adjacent or widely separated points on the same metal caused by varying distribution of alloys, varying stress distribution, or varying oxygen concentrations on the surface due to dirt, crevices, contacting materials, or variations in the seawater velocity.

TABLE 4-1   Galvanic series for metals and alloys in flowing seawater. (Adapted from Tuthill and Schillmoller 1965.)

Magnesium	
Zinc	Least Noble ↑
Beryllium	
Aluminum	
Cadmium	
Mild Steel	
Low Alloy Steel	
Cast Iron	
Type 410, Stainless Steel (Active)	
Type 430, Stainless Steel (Active)	
Type 304, Stainless Steel (Active)	
Type 316, Stainless Steel (Active)	
Ni-Resist Cast Iron	
Aluminum Bronze	
Yellow Brass	
Tin	
Copper	
Admiralty Brass	
Aluminum Brass	
Manganese Bronze	
Silicon Bronze	
Tin Bronze	
Type 410 (Passive)	
Type 430 (Passive)	
90/10 Copper-Nickel	
Lead	
70/30 Copper-Nickel	
Silver Braze Alloys	
Nickel	
Inconel	Most Noble
Silver	↓
Type 304 (Passive)	
Type 316 (Passive)	
Monel	
Hastelloy C	
Titanium	
Platinum	
Graphite	

Types of corrosion encountered in seawater include uniform attack, pitting corrosion, concentration cells, intergranular corrosion, stress corrosion, and corrosion fatigue. Uniform attack or general corrosion may or may not present a problem. A coating of rust on a steel shaft can quickly seize up a mechanism. However, a light oxide coating formed on many materials, such as titanium, chromium, and nickel, actually protect the metal from further corrosion. These materials are said to become passive or exhibit passivity because of the formation of the protective film. It is such a passive film that imparts the desirable corrosion-resistant properties to the austenitic (300 series) stainless steels.

When a metal receives its corrosion protection from a passive oxide film, anything that breaks up or reduces the film in a local area can greatly accelerate corrosion by forming a corrosion cell between the active point and the remainder of the passive surface. Pitting is an example of localized corrosion that occurs when protective films or layers of corrosion product break down. Pits are very serious in tool and manipulator components because they concentrate the attack over a small area and can act as stress concentrations. Austenitic stainless steels are particularly susceptible to pitting corrosion, particularly in quiet (nonmoving) seawater where the oxygen needed to passivate a surface quickly depletes.

Concentration cell corrosion is a general name given to the type of corrosion where local differences in oxygen, temperature, agitation, liquid velocity, or any other heterogeneric condition sets up a small corrosion cell. Pitting is one example of a concentration cell, but the most common one in seawater is crevice corrosion, which generally occurs where two pieces mate or a seal contacts a metal. Austenitic and ferritic stainless steels are very susceptible to crevice corrosion, while titanium, the copper-nickels, and the Inconels generally are not.

Intergranular corrosion is a selective attack along a metal's grain boundaries that can result in intercrystalline cracking. It occurs most often in underwater applications where certain austenitic stainless steels are welded and not properly heat treated. Intergranular corrosion can be avoided through the use of the extra-low-carbon austenitic alloys (Types 304L and 316L are examples), proper heat treating, or selection of a stabilized grade (Types 321 and 347 are examples).

Stress corrosion cracking can occur in many metals subjected to high stresses. Localized corrosion tends to concentrate at points of high stress and form pits or trenches that cause high stress concentration or lead to premature, often catastrophic failure. Materials particularly susceptible to stress corrosion include the 2000 and 7000 series of high-strength aluminums, high-strength steels, and precipitation-hardening stainless steels when not stress relieved to at least 1100°F (590°C). Corrosion fatigue works in the same manner as stress corrosion to concentrate corrosion at high-stress points in cyclic-loaded pieces, causing metal failure or loads substantially below the fatigue limit for noncorrosive conditions.

Aluminum alloys have some special corrosion vulnerabilities of which users should be aware. One of the chief problems is that the corrosion performance of aluminum alloys can be influenced markedly by the presence of trace amounts of certain impurities in the water in which they are immersed. The most notable harmful impurity is the copper ion, small traces of which will cause rapid aluminum corrosion. Allied to this effect is the fact that mere proximity of copper metal or copper alloys to aluminum alloys in seawater will cause rapid attack on the aluminum even though the two metals may be electrically isolated from each other. The attack in the latter case is also caused by the presence of copper ions in the water adjacent to the aluminum alloy, the copper ions originating from the corrosion of the copper. The reason for the deleterious effect of copper ions is that the copper ions are able to plate out (copper being more noble than aluminum) on the aluminum surface. After this has happened, galvanic corrosion can take place with the copper deposits acting as cathodes. (Copper and aluminum form an especially powerful galvanic couple [see Table 4-1]; the use of these two metals in the same equipment in seawater should be undertaken with great caution.) As noted in the protective coatings section later in this chapter, aluminum alloys can be fairly well protected by hard-coat anodizing for short-term immersion, or by hard-coat anodizing and painting or Teflon impregnating the surface for long-term immersion.

In the selection of materials for underwater tools, there are several general rules to follow.

1. If possible, make the tool from one metal, and select as noble a metal as possible within the other design constraints.

2. When using multiple alloys, make key components, such as fasteners and rotating components, more noble so that they are protected by the more cathodic parts. Choose metals that are close together in the galvanic series, if possible.

3. Allow for increased corrosion of the less noble (more anodic) components by providing larger surface areas. If this is not possible, it may be necessary to "mask" the more corrosion-resistant (cathodic) materials by coating with paint or grease.

4. Avoid the use of plastics and elastomerics in contact with materials (such as austenitic stainless steel) that are sensitive to concentration cells.

5. Where possible, consider cathodically protecting the tool by adding a sacrificial anode of zinc or of another suitable alloy.

6. Protect mating surfaces and fasteners with corrosion-resistant greases and lubricants. (Zinc oxide, NEVERSEEZ[R], and AQUA-LUBE[R] are examples.)

Plastics and Elastomers

Plastics and elastomers are particularly resistant to deterioration by sea-water (see Table 4-2). In addition, they are lightweight, with some being nearly neutral in water. As a result, many plastics are being extensively used on underwater equipment, particularly on submersibles. Although glass-reinforced plastics have been considered for some structural components for underwater tools and manipulators, plastic use to date has primarily been limited to seals, covers, wear surfaces, springs, and bearings.

As will be discussed in more detail in Chapter 5, care must be taken in designing seals to ensure that the design accommodates the material changes that can occur at depth. The cold temperatures and increased pressure at depth can result in an increase in friction and a decrease in seal size. In addition, the seal design must have no trapped cavities into which the seal can extrude at high ambient pressures. When elastomeric seals are specified for deep applications, a material hardness of 90 durometer is usually specified to minimize size and volume change.

Protective Coatings

Protective coatings are used extensively to protect metals from rapid deterioration in seawater. Various types of paint systems, including epoxy and organic paints, are used extensively on commercially available hand tools. All paint systems, however, require continued maintenance to keep a sound, defect-free coating. In fact, for many materials a defect in a painted surface can result in a concentration cell and accelerated corrosion.

Next to paint, anodize coatings are probably the most widely used coatings. As a minimum, most aluminum tools are hard-coat anodized with a 0.002-inch-thick (0.05 mm) coating to prevent general corrosion from forming. Some tools are painted after anodizing to further increase the protection, but a fairly recent development of Teflon^R-impregnated anodize surfaces is proving to be extremely effective in corrosion prevention and may eliminate the need to paint. Up to 5 years of intermittent service in seawater without corrosion has been reported for these types of coatings. It is especially important in designing aluminum parts that they be hard anodized to provide for a 0.001-inch (0.025-mm) increase in each surface dimension for each 0.002 inch (0.05 mm) of coating. In addition, all corners should have at least a 0.010-inch (0.25-mm) radius.

If properly applied, chromium coatings can be used very effectively to protect tool steels on wear surfaces and shafts. The chromium plate should be at least 0.001 inch (0.025 mm) thick and should not have a flash coating

TABLE 4-2 Resistance of plastics and elastomers to deterioration.

	Acetal Copolymer (Delrin R)	Acrylic (Plexiglas R)	Butyl Rubber	Buna N	Epoxy	Polyethylene	Polypropylene	Polyurethane	Polyvinyl Chloride	Natural Rubber	Neoprene	Nylon	Silicon Rubber	TFE (Teflon R)	Viton R
Oxidation	U	U	E	G	U	E	U	G	U	F	G	U	E	E	E
Petroleum Oil	E	F	X	E	E	E	X	G	X	X	G	E	F	E	E
Seawater	E	E	E	E	E	E	E	F	E	E	G	E	E	E	E
Silicon Oil	U	U	E	E	E	U	U	E	U	U	E	E	E	E	E
Sunlight	E	E	G	U	G	X	X	G	G	F	G	G	E	E	U
Water	E	E	E	E	E	E	E	F	E	E	G	E	E	E	E

E = Excellent
G = Good
F = Fair
U = Unknown
X = Not Recommended

93

or a layer of nickel applied prior to applying the chromium. It is a common misconception that chromium coatings will not hold up in seawater; in fact, chromium will last very well on parts that have a good surface finish and no sharp corners or crevices. It is important that only a single layer of chromium be applied.

Many components have also been protected by electroplating with zinc and cadium. Generally, these do not provide sufficient protection for long-term immersion and can form deteriorative corrosion products on tools. However, some tools and many manipulators have been protected with well-placed zinc anodes, as discussed in the next section.

Cathodic Protection

Cathodic protection of immersed systems involves supplying a cathodic current to the structure either by attaching an anodic (sacrificial) material to it, or by impressing an electric current on the structure from a power supply and using an insoluble anode. In the former case, the technique may be looked upon as a constructive application of galvanic corrosion. Sacrificial anodes have traditionally been zinc, but in recent years aluminum and magnesium anodes have also been used.

Cathodic protection is obtained when the electrical potential of a structure (such as a ship's hull) is reduced to a particular value, specific to the material. The electrical potential is an electrode potential measurable with a reference electrode placed in the water close to the structure. (For steel, the potential required for protection is -0.85 V versus a $Cu/CuSO_4$ reference electrode.) This point is stressed because it is sometimes thought that cathodic protection is obtained when a cathodic current is supplied all over the structure—that is, that net current direction alone is a sufficient condition. However, current-density values for protection of a given material are variable, but the protection potential does not vary. For instance, a much greater current density is generally required to obtain the protection potential in moving water than in still water.

In undersea work, cathodic protection is applied to steel and to aluminum alloys. Cathodic protection of steel is well understood and has a good theoretical basis (which is often used as the example in texts on cathodic protection). However, although many aluminum alloys can be cathodically protected (with zinc anodes, for instance), there is no rigorous theoretical basis for this since substantial protection is obtained at potentials well above the theoretical protection potential for aluminum. In fact, aluminum alloys can be overprotected by applying the theoretical protection potential to aluminum, resulting in caustic corrosion.

For optimum coverage, anodes should be placed so that there is a straight line current path between an anode and all parts of the structure to be protected. Anodes do not protect a surface well from general corrosion when the surface is around a corner from an anode, although some protection from crevice corrosion may occur.

The amount of anode required to obtain protection can be accurately quantified for steel, and is shown on sales literature on the anode material. The requirement is specified in terms of anode surface area versus steel surface area. (The mass of anode used is important primarily in that it affects the replacement frequency.) The amount of anode area required to protect aluminum alloys is not available in the literature, which reflects the fact that cathodic protection of aluminum is not well understood.

One form of zinc anode that is especially useful in protecting small or intricate systems is "Diamond Line" made by the American Smelting and Refining Company (ASARCO). It is sometimes referred to as a ribbon-type anode and is supplied in coil form so that convenient lengths can be cut for a particular installation. It is available in three different diamond-shaped cross sections ranging in size from 0.34 × 0.48 inches (8.7 × 11.9 mm) to 0.62 × 0.88 inches (16 × 22 mm). The diamond-shaped cross section contains a 0.1-inch-diameter (2.5 mm) steel-core wire. The steel-core wire is exposed at both ends and is used to make electrical and mechanical connections with the structure to be protected. In the case of a steel structure, the connection is best made by welding. For an aluminum alloy structure, stainless steel ground lugs or binding posts can be threaded into the aluminum alloy. An especially useful feature of Diamond Line is its flexibility, which makes it useful for attachment to structures that are already designed and where a protection system must be improvised. It is also useful in complex structures, such as manipulator arms, that contain many small recesses and projections.

Impressed current systems are used to protect all-steel structures. Insoluble anodes such as Pb-Ag and Pt-Ti are used in these systems. The systems can be supplied at two levels of sophistication: (1) with manual adjustment of current density on the structure; and (2) with automatic adjustment of current density by means of controlling reference electrodes. These reference electrodes are installed at one or more locations close to the protected structure to measure its potential. Any departure from the ideal protection potential is sensed, and the associated signal is used to automatically adjust the current. Automatic current adjustment is desirable on a ship's hull since the current density required to maintain the protection potential varies with speed.

The alkalinity associated with cathodic reactions will generally lead to formation of a calcareous coating on a cathodically protected structure in natural seawater. The coating consists of a mixture of $CaCO_3$ and $Mg(OH)_2$. The coating can be visible under some circumstances, building up to a cement-like layer. The formation of the coating is protective in itself and reduces the current required for cathodic protection since, once formed, current is needed only to protect the holes in the coating (which are gradually plugged with additional calcareous deposits). Intentional use is made of the calcareous coating in many off-shore structures used in the oil industry. In these structures, an especially heavy protective current-density is applied for a short time after installation in order to build up a calcareous deposit ("prepolarization"). Thereafter, only a small amount of current is required for protection, since it is only necessary to supply enough current to keep the coating repaired.

PRESSURE COMPENSATION

Equipment used underwater must be capable of withstanding the external pressure of the water at its intended depth of operation. Discounting the effects of temperature, salinity, and increased density at depth due to bulk modulus changes, the ambient pressure of seawater at depth increases approximately 0.444 lb per square inch per ft (10kPa/m) of depth. Myers Holm, and McAllister (1969) recommend using the following formula for estimating the pressure at the operating depth:

$$p = 0.444h + 0.3 \left(\frac{h}{1000}\right)^2$$

where

   h = depth of seawater in feet

and

   p = ambient pressure at depth h in pounds per square inch

This formula yields the gage pressure (add atmospheric pressure for the absolute pressure) and includes the effect of density changes at depth due to bulk modulus effects.

Equipment that is sensitive to pressure or seawater, such as electrical controls, electronic equipment, and batteries, is often housed in watertight capsules for use in the ocean. As the operating depth increases, the wall thickness of the capsule can become so thick or the sealing problems (such as for rotating shafts) can become so difficult that the equipment is not practical. Figure 4-1 shows the ratio of wall thickness to diameter versus collapse depth for various materials. At great depths, even such small "trapped" volumes as the cavity under a bolt in a blind tapped hole can be damaged or collapsed unless they are pressure compensated in some manner.

Pressure compensation of equipment for deep submergence use can be

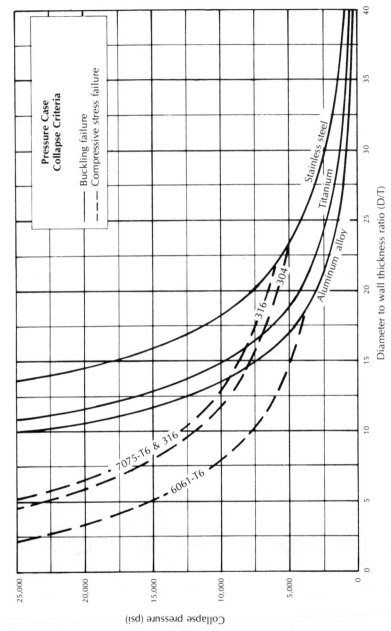

FIGURE 4-1 Collapse pressure versus diameter-to-wall-thickness ratio for cylinders. (Courtesy of InterOceans Systems, Inc., San Diego, California.)

accomplished by filling voids or air spaces with fluid and exposing the fluid to the ambient pressure at depth. The compensating fluid used may be seawater itself for such cavities as blind tapped holes that can be cross drilled to expose them to the ambient pressure. However, most pressure compensation is provided by filling the cavity with oil and using various devices, such as a diaphragm, bellows, piston, or bladder, to provide a moving interface between the compensating fluid and seawater (Mehneit 1972). This moving interface is necessary to allow for the change in oil volume due to changes in temperature and ambient pressure (bulk modulus effects). Often the moving interface is spring loaded to provide a slightly higher internal pressure than external pressure so that any leakage tends to be outward from the cavity, thereby preventing seawater intrusion.

If the seawater-to-fluid pressure differentials are kept to a minimum using pressure compensation, the equipment size, cost, and often complexity can be kept to a minimum. This is especially important for tools and manipulators used with submersibles where weight must be minimized to control the size and cost of flotation. Also, minimal differential pressure across enclosure penetrations and associated seals simplifies their design. Static or dynamic sealing does, however, take on a unique design requirement—that of providing a low differential pressure seal in a cyclic high-ambient pressure environment. Compensating fluids can also assist in heat transfer from electronic or hydraulic components and can inhibit seawater corrosion. In addition, thin-walled enclosures are often more readily disassembled for equipment inspection, troubleshooting, and maintenance. Hard-shell nonpressure-compensated capsules do offer the advantage that the components are not subjected to pressure cycling, which is often important for electronic components, and that hard-shell systems do not require filling, draining, and cleaning.

Inner tubes, elastomeric hoses, flexible bags, rubber bags from hydraulic oil accumulators, rolling diaphragms, metal bellows, elastomeric bellows, piston-cylinder arrangements, and flat and convoluted diaghragms have all been used to provide the variable volume capability required for pressure compensation. In determining the variable volume capacity needed, the designer must allow for the variation in fluid temperatures expected, the amount of entrapped and/or dissolved gas in fluid, the bulk modulus effects of the fluid, any volume variations due to actuator motions, and leakage. Typical temperature design ranges are −40 to 140°F (−40 to 60°C) for transportation and 28 to 90°F (−2 to 32°C) for operation in water. A rule of the thumb often used is to provide a variable volume equal to ½ percent of the nominal volume per 1000 psi (6900 kPa) ambient pressure, plus a minimum of 10 percent to account for temperature extremes (5 percent) and leakage (5 percent), plus the amount required to compensate for any actuator motions. Thus, a device for use at 20,000 ft

(6100 m) should have a minimum of 15 percent compensation volume. In heavily used systems, systems with many components, or systems requiring extreme reliability, compensation volumes 2 to 3 times those calculated by this method are often used to provide a significant operating time even when a slow leak occurs.

Pressure-compensated systems should be designed such that system low points contain fill/drain ports and system high points have ports for venting or filling. Seawater detectors can be installed in system low points to provide warning of seawater intrusion. Low-pressure spring-loaded check valves are often used to relieve internal overpressure, especially during filling, and are also used to admit seawater in some systems to prevent collapse of the enclosure should the system compensating fluid become depleted, as can be caused by a seal failure in a hydraulic system. Pressure-relief valves are often used to relieve trapped fluid in "locked-off" portions of hydraulic systems during large depth excursions.

5

COMPONENT SELECTION

IN the interest of economy, underwater work systems are configured from as many commercially available components as is practical. Often the selection is a compromise between what is readily available and what is desirable from a standpoint of long-term use. This chapter supplements the more general discussions of the previous two chapters with specific details concerning the selection and modification of hydraulic components, seals, and tool bits for use in underwater applications.

HYDRAULIC COMPONENTS

As discussed in Chapter 3, hydraulic tools use flowing oil under pressure to actuate a mechanical output device. In most cases, the mechanical output device is a linear or rotary actuator or a hydraulic motor. The flow of the oil to the output device is directed by directional-control valves and regulated in pressure and flow by pressure-control and flow-control valves. Often these valves are packaged in a separate enclosure to protect them from the corrosive seawater environment, thus allowing the use of conventional hydraulic components. A brief discussion of the various types of hydraulic components follows, with emphasis upon their underwater application.

Linear Actuators

Linear actuators offer high force capability, high power per weight and size, and ease of speed control in both directions. Although bellows, diaphragm, and rolling diaphragm actuators have all been used under-water, the piston-type linear actuator (usually called a hydraulic-cylinder actuator) is most commonly used. Hydraulic-cylinder actuators offer good mechanical stiffness and high speed of response, provide longer strokes, and permit higher pressues than bellows or diaphragm actuators. However, piston actuators do have greater drag and friction than other linear actuators. Piston-actuated tools were shown in Figures 2-9, 2-15, and 2-16. Commercially available high-pressure hydraulic cylinders are usu-ally all-steel in construction, with the exceptions of the piston and the rod-guide bearing, which are usually constructed with bearing bronze or nodular iron to prevent corrosion.

In many cases the cylinder body is cold-drawn MT 1020 steel tubing with the bore honed to a high finish and hard chrome plated. Hard-coated, cold-drawn aluminum-alloy tubing is now being used successfully as cylinder body material for air and hydraulic cylinders having small bores. Heat-treated alloy steels are used for hydraulic cylinders of very high pressure to keep weight within reasonable limits and to maintain a suffi-cient factor of safety. Hydraulic cylinders designed for commercial water-based hydraulic fluids usually have bronze or brass cylinder bodies, bronze or stainless steel pistons, and cadmium- or electroless-nickel-plated heads. If the actuator is a tie-rod type, the tie rods are usually steel of high tensile strength. The cylinder rods are generally chrome-plated steel.

The commercially available cylinders often are used directly in seawater for short-term uses without modification. However, if the use is to be relatively continuous, the body and tie rods are usually painted with a good grade of marine paint, and chrome-plated stainless steel rods are used. Even with these precautions, however, corrosion often occurs in locations such as voids, chips, or cracks in the paint (called holidays) or in the chrome plating after only a few dives or a few weeks of continuous immersion. When long-term immersion or limited maintenance is neces-sary, the hydraulic cylinders generally are specially made, such as the one shown in Figure 5-1. In these cases the bodies and rods are often 316 stainless steel, a high-strength, precipitation-harding stainless, or Inconel. In addition, for long-term use the bore and rod may be hard chrome plated and ground to a smooth finish. The degree of finish, especially on the cylinder bore, piston rod, piston, and rod-guide bushing, affects the life of

Port fittings   Cylinder   Cap

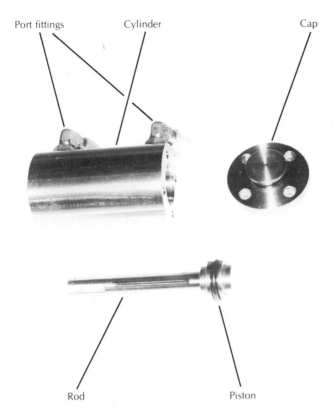

Rod   Piston

FIGURE 5-1   All-stainless-steel hydraulic cylinder.

the cylinder, piston, and rod seals. A finish of 8 microinches is the maximum roughness allowable for any of these parts.

When long-term immersion and high reliability are required, two rod seals in series are sometimes used—with the cavity between the seals connected to the return. Thus, any oil leakage outward across the high-pressure seal is returned to the reservoir and any water leakage inward is returned to the reservoir, by-passing sensitive components such as servo-valves. Also, in long-term immersion, zinc inserts have been used between the rod wiper and rod seal to anodically protect any internal voids from corrosion. Rod wipers or scrapers are necessary for cylinders that operate in environments where dirt and grit can accumulate on the exposed cylinder rod, which is often the case underwater. Whenever possible, the tool should be designed such that the rod is retracted when not in use. This design will greatly lengthen the life of chrome-plated rods.

There is a considerable effort underway to develop seawater hydraulic systems in which seawater is used directly as the hydraulic fluid. Hydraulic cylinders are probably the most applicable hydraulic components for use with seawater because of their simple parts and lack of tight tolerances in lower-pressure cylinders. However, none of the commercially available hydraulic cylinder materials to date will hold up when continuously filled with seawater. Only specialized ceramics, titanium, or the more exotic alloys will last under continuous-use conditions; such cylinders would have to be specially made.

In designing special cylinders for underwater use, care must be taken to prevent excessive side forces from damaging the cylinder. When the cylinder is fully extended, only the length of the piston bearing and the rod bearing combined is available to resist the overturning moment caused by lateral side forces. The rod-bearing length added to piston-bearing length, plus the space between the two bearings when the cylinder is fully extended, should not be less than three times the rod diameter, but should be equal to or larger than the bore of the cylinder. This distance, which is the moment arm supporting the sagging moment of an extended piston rod, can be increased by the use of stop tubes inside the cylinder body. Stop tubes prevent the piston from going all the way to the head end of the cylinder, thereby sacrificing stroke length for rigidity.

The most important consideration in rod diameter is whether the main force acts on the rod in tension, or compression, or both. If the force acts on the rod in tension only, the rod diameter needs to be only large enough to take the cylinder force. Because of its length, an actuator cannot be held in a straight line under compressive loads. A slight eccentric loading always occurs, causing bending stresses in addition to the compressive stresses. Thus, the rod must be large enough in diameter to prevent buckling when used in compression. Piston-rod diameter also affects the piston velocity and force of a single-rod end cylinder. If the piston rod has a 2:1 differential area (area of piston rod equal to one-half the cylinder area), the return stroke is twice as fast as the extension stroke for constant inlet flow. However, this differential area reduces the cylinder force by one-half on the return stroke for a given working pressure. In single-rod end cylinders, the change in internal volume of the oil within the cylinder must be considered when sizing a pressure compensator. If this volume change is critical, double-rod end cylinders can be used.

The maximum pressure that hydraulic cylinders can safely withstand is often far below the bursting pressure of the cylinder wall. For example, allowable pressure may be limited by the ability of the seals to operate with the increased clearances caused by cylinder-wall deformation or by tie-rod stretch. If, because of excessive fluid pressure, the clearance between the piston and the cylinder wall becomes greater than the piston seal's ability to withstand extrusion, the seal will fail prematurely. This increase in cylinder diameter must be carefully considered in hydraulic cylinder design where a pump of very high pressure is used. Unless packaging a large-diameter cylinder is a problem, a lighter system may result when a larger-diameter, lower-pressure cylinder is used in place of a small-diameter, high-pressure system. Seal design handbooks, such as those provided by the Parker Seal Company, offer a considerable amount of design information concerning the use of all types of seals. Elastomers provide the most efficient sealing on lubricated shafts or bores, but no presently available economical material is compatible with all common hydraulic fluids. Fluorcarbon rubber (such as DuPont's Viton[R] and 3M's Fluorel[R]) is the most commonly used compound today that is compatible with petroleum, water, water-glycol, and most phosphate-esterbase fluids, as well as with elevated temperatures (see Table 4-2).

Hydraulic Motors

Hydraulic motors convert hydraulic fluid flow into rotary motion and pressure into load torque. Pressure drop across a motor will never exceed the amount required to accelerate the load or keep it running at a constant speed. The hydraulic motors used in underwater tools are usually positive-displacement gear or piston-type motors. Vane motors have not been widely used in underwater applications.

Positive-displacement fluid motors are hydrostatic devices. Their theoretical speed is determined by flow rate and is independent of load. Their theoretical torque is independent of design type and is determined by pressure and displacement:

$$\text{torque (lbf-inch)} = \frac{\text{Pressure (psi)} \times \text{displacement (inch}^3\text{/rev)}}{2\pi}$$

$$\text{theoretical speed (rpm)} = \frac{231 \times \text{flow (gpm)}}{\text{displacement (inch}^3\text{/rev)}}$$

Advantages of positive-displacement fluid motors over competing means of power transmission include their small size, high power-to-weight ratio, easily controlled speed, easily controlled torque, dynamic braking capability, and easily reversed rotation. As with hydraulic cylinders, commercially available motors are often used directly in seawater with only the addition of a more corrosion-resistant paint. However, frequently the rotating group (the working component) from a commercially available motor is placed in a specifically designed corrosion-resistant housing.

Gear Motors.   Gear motors are the least expensive and most forgiving of the positive-displacement motors. The four most significant types of gear motors are the gear-on-gear, gear-within-gear, differential gear, and crescent (Meisel 1972). All have a fixed geometry (displacement) hydraulic unbalance and fairly short leakage paths, which lead to poor overall efficiency in comparison with piston motors.

In the simplest gear motor, the gear-on-gear type, a pair of matched gears are enclosed in a case (see Figure 5-2). The inlet and outlet ports are located in either the sides or the axial faces of the case. The motor displaces fluid between the tooth spaces and the outer wall. One-half of the delivered torque is transmitted through the tooth engagement to the gear with the shaft attached.

Some gear motors provide for axial retainment and sealing of the gears with pressure-loaded wear plates. Pressure from the ports is directed to select portions on the outside of the wear plates. This slightly overbalances the internal pressure forces and reduces the leakage past the gear faces to a

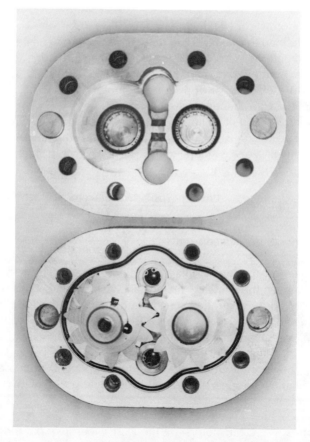

FIGURE 5-2 Internal view of a typical gear-on-gear motor.

minimum. Gear-on-gear motors are rated at pressures to 3,000 psi (21 MPa). However, relatively high leakage at those pressures reduces the overall efficiency and the accuracy of speed control, and must be considered in their application.

Because of their light weight, low cost, and convenient package size, all commercially available diving tools use gear-on-gear motors. Gear-within-gear motors (often called Gerotor® motors after a popular brand) work such that they have a built-in 7-to-1 or 9-to-1 reduction, thereby making them highly desirable for lower-speed, higher-torque applications.

Piston Motors.   Piston motors are commercially available in both radial piston and axial piston configurations. Radial piston motors have the pistons oriented radially from the output shaft, and tend to be used only in very large motors. An inline axial piston motor contains a rotating barrel with several pistons (generally 7 or 9) parallel to its axis (see Figures 5-3 and 5-4). The barrel drives the output shaft through a splined joint. Pressurized

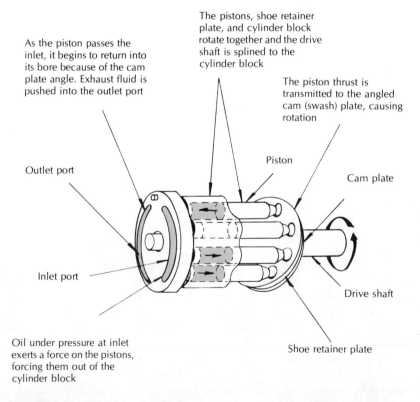

The pistons, shoe retainer plate, and cylinder block rotate together and the drive shaft is splined to the cylinder block

As the piston passes the inlet, it begins to return into its bore because of the cam plate angle. Exhaust fluid is pushed into the outlet port

The piston thrust is transmitted to the angled cam (swash) plate, causing rotation

Outlet port

Piston

Cam plate

Inlet port

Drive shaft

Oil under pressure at inlet exerts a force on the pistons, forcing them out of the cylinder block

Shoe retainer plate

FIGURE 5-3 Inline axial piston motor operation.

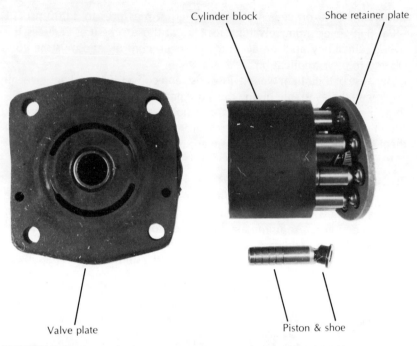

Cylinder block   Shoe retainer plate

Valve plate   Piston & shoe

FIGURE 5-4 Typical inline axial piston motor components.

fluid enters either of the external ports and is passed through the port face of the barrel to the piston cavities, causing the pistons to extend. The pistons are restrained at the opposite end by a sloping cam plate down which they ride, rotating the barrel as they rotate. The extended end of the piston terminates in a ball to which is swaged a shoe that bears against the cam plate. When fully extended, the piston cavity is sealed from the pressurized fluid port and is exhausted through the fluid outlet port. The piston is then returned to the fully retracted position, and the power stroke repeats. The angle of the cam plate determines motor displacement, and may be fixed or variable.

This design lends itself to a balance of the various pressure forces within the motor and allows continuous operating pressures to 5,000 psi (34 MPa). For instance, the shoes have relieved areas that are pressurized through a hole from the cylinder. This pressure creates a hydrostatic bearing for the normal forces acting through the cam plate. The summation of the radial components of those normal forces can be carried through a bearing at the balance point on the barrel; this eliminates the need of high clamping-pressure forces and bearing loads to keep the barrel sealing against the port surface. No thrust bearings are required in this design.

Inline axial piston motors have very high volumetric efficiencies, and are excellent for high-speed operation. However, high friction at low speeds usually limits their usefulness for continuous operation below 50 rpm. As with the gear motor, the shape of inline axial piston motors lends them to convenient repackaging into corrosion-resistant bodies.

Another type of axial piston motor has a bent axis on which the barrel rotates (see Figures 5-5 and 5-6). The piston thrust is delivered through ball links to a retainer attached to the output shaft. Piston force is unbalanced and is supported on thrust bearings. A double universal link keeps the barrel rotating with the shaft; this link is subjected to very small torsional loads under steady-speed conditions, but is severely stressed under dynamic conditions.

The bent-axis piston motor has the same efficiency and advantages as the inline motor. Because of reduced friction at low speeds, it is more suitable for continuous operation to as low as 20 rpm. In battery-operated vehicles when power is limited, the higher efficiency piston motors are usually used rather than the less efficient gear motors.

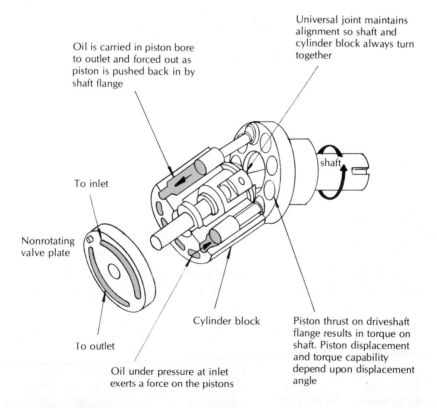

FIGURE 5-5   Bent-axis piston motor operation.

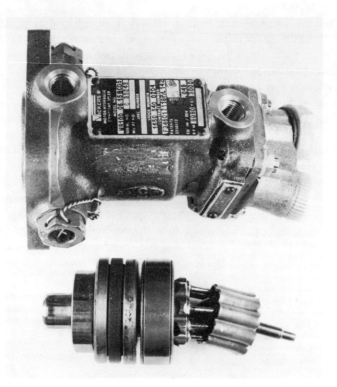

FIGURE 5-6 Typical bent-axis piston motor.

Rotary Actuators

Rotary actuators rotate an output shaft through a fixed arc, as opposed to a continuous rotation like that of a hydraulic motor. Rotary actuators are compact and offer a high torque capability in a simple, easily mounted housing. The primary underwater use of rotary actuators has been for actuating rotary joints in manipulators. There are two basic types of actuators—vane and piston. Both types are positive displacement, but the vane type is usually lighter in weight for a given torque capacity. However, while piston actuators are generally considered leak-free, the vane type typically exhibits a small amount of leakage under load. This prevents vane-actuated devices from holding position under load without using a servo loop or an external locking means. In addition, vane actuators are limited in rotational arc to about 280 degrees for a single-vane unit and 100 degrees for a double-vane unit, and are usually limited in pressure capability to about 1000 psi (7 MPa).

There are several different types of piston-type actuators, including helical spline, piston-rack, and piston-chain actuators. However, the piston-rack is the only type that has been used extensively underwater. Piston-rack actuators are essentially leak-free and can be used to hold loads without external means by simply blocking off hydraulic flow.

Many rotary actuators can be purchased in anodized aluminum with acceptable rotary shaft seals for underwater use. However, in deep applications care must be taken to ensure that all sealed volumes are pressure compensated, especially the pinion housing. Often these volumes are connected to the reservoir return line.

Hydraulic Valves

Hydraulic valves are used to control the flow into and out of the output device, to protect the device from overpressure, and to control the torque or force output of the device. In many cases, commercially available hydraulic valves are used in underwater applications without modification. However, they are generally housed in a protective enclosure usually called a valve package. The valve package is usually oil filled and pressure compensated for deep ocean uses. Because the internal working parts of commercial valves are usually common steel machined or ground to a bright finish, they are very vulnerable to damage if seawater enters the circuit and is not quickly flushed from the components. Since there will always be a small amount of seawater seeping into any working system, it is important to use a hydraulic oil with corrosion inhibitors. In many systems, the valve package is protected with a different oil compensator than the actual hydraulic system so that there is less chance of seawater intrusion into the electrical coils of the valves.

Direction-Control Valves.   Direction-control valves provide a means for controlling when and where fluid is delivered to perform various functions. The valves start, stop, accelerate, decelerate, and control the direction of motion of actuators and motors. They can be used to hold the actuator in a fixed position or to cause it to move in either direction. Direction-control valves are classified as two-way, three-way, or four-way to indicate the type of circuit to which they are applied; the number is determined by the number of ports the valve can pressurize and exhaust.

Two-way and three-way direction-control valves have only two operating positions, while most four-way directional-control valves have either two or three operating positions. A three-position valve can be used to hold an actuator in an intermediate position, provide a path for fluid back to the tank while the actuator is not being moved in either direction, or isolate an actuator from the rest of the circuit while it is not being operated. Although there are many operating configurations, most four-way direction-control valves use a sliding spool to control flow. In a typical three-position, electrically controlled valve, the spool is spring-centered while the solenoids are de-energized. When either solenoid is energized, the spool is moved against the opposite spring. The two-position spool valve is normally held in one position by spring force and shifted to the alternate position by the actuation device. The spring returns the valve to its normal position when the actuation force is removed.

The spool configuration and the method of actuation determine the valve function. The major types of spool valves are open center, closed center, and tandem, although many other configurations are available (see Figure 5-7). These designations refer to the configuration of spool in the center position; the symbols used in Figure 5-7 indicate spring-centered, solenoid-operated valves.

Small solenoid-operated valves (less than about 10 gpm) are generally single stage and operate by direct action of a solenoid plunger on the valve spool. Larger valves are usually a combination of a pilot valve mounted on another valve that contains a larger spool, and are referred to as solenoid-controlled, pilot-operated valves. The required flow determines the need for a single-stage or two-stage valve. Solenoids are commercially available in a variety of voltages, both ac and dc. Electrical characteristics of ac solenoids include both in-rush and holding-type currents. A typical 115-V solenoid may have an in-rush current of 3.6 A and a holding current of only 0.6 A. Thus, the in-rush current must be accommodated by the wire size and control system electronics of the underwater system. There have been many cases in underwater equipment where the failure of a valve to operate was traced to not using a large enough wire and power supply to carry the in-rush current.

Manually operated valves provide throttling control in response to an operator's movement of a handle. They are often used to control part of a sequence of events in which the time elements are not precise and the operator must initiate the required action. In some uses, the operating lever is replaced by a roller or suitable linkage to provide a method of limiting or sequencing work system operations.

Most commercially available valves are not capable of use directly immersed in seawater except for very short periods of time. Generally the solenoids and spring-return mechanisms are not sealed from water and the external components are not corrosion resistant. In addition, many valves, especially some poppet-type three-way valves, have trapped volumes that limit the operational depth without rework.

Spool-type valves have the desirable feature that the spool leakage prevents uncompensated trapped volumes from occurring. However, they have the undesirable feature that they will not support fixed loads in positive displacement devices without adding pilot-operated port checks

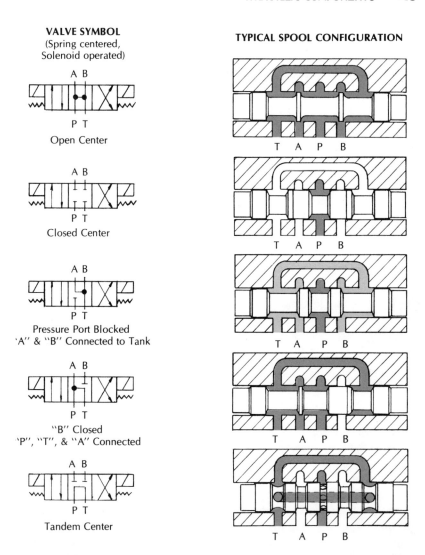

VALVE SYMBOL
(Spring centered,
Solenoid operated)

A B

P T

Open Center

A B

P T

Closed Center

A B

P T

Pressure Port Blocked
'A'' & ''B'' Connected to Tank

A B

P T

''B'' Closed
'P'', ''T'', & ''A'' Connected

A B

P T

Tandem Center

TYPICAL SPOOL CONFIGURATION

T   A   P   B

T   A   P   B

T   A   P   B

T   A   P   B

T   A   P   B

FIGURE 5-7   Typical three-position, four-way valve configurations.

or lock blocks. One manufacturer of underwater valves gets around this dilemma by using a specially designed poppet-type three-way valve with a balanced poppet and soft seat seals for zero spool leakage. By properly manifolding two three-way valves, an open-center four-way valve results. With the addition of a lock block, the valves can be used in a closed-center mode. Figure 5-8 shows a schematic of how this is done. However, caution must be taken to ensure that the trapped volumes are compensated during ascent from or descent to deep depths.

The solenoid operators must also be checked to ensure that they will

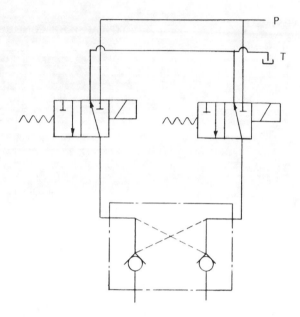

FIGURE 5-8   Schematic of a closed-center four-way valve created by using two
three-way valves with a lock block.

operate properly and not be damaged at pressure. If the coil is potted, there
can be voids that may collapse at depth and damage the coil. It is good
practice to cycle test all valves at ambient pressures equivalent to the
system design depth prior to use and to proof test the potted coils by
pressuring to 1½ times the design depth for 10 cycles.

Servovalves.   Solenoid-actuated directional-control valves can only be
actuated full stroke when the solenoid is energized resulting in full-speed
motion of the actuator. When it is necessary to provide a variable velocity,
acceleration, or position, an electrohydraulic servovalve, usually simply
called a servovalve, can be used. Servovalves provide hydraulic output
proportional to electrical input. Servovalves are used in many underwater
applications, including proportional control of thruster speed on submersibles and accurate control of mechanical position in manipulators. Most
servovalves used are the two-stage type in which a torque motor or moving
coil actuates a pilot spool, jet pipe, or flapper valve, which in turn shifts a
main spool. The main spool is usually a four-way spool, although three-
way units are available for specific applications.

  Servovalves have a reputation for being somewhat unreliable in underwater applications primarily because of their susceptibility to damage by
dirt. Of the various types, the jet-pipe pilot is the most resistant to contami-

nation. It is important to design circuits using servovalves so that they can be cleaned easily and so that all return oil and oil leaving the pump is filtered through 10-micron filters. Another important item to note is that all but one type of servovalve draw a continuous pilot flow. Typically this flow is about 0.1 gpm (6 cm³/sec). In some applications involving several servovalves, the pilot flow required for the system is more than the maximum flow in any single circuit. Also, when the servovalves are not under power, the actuators can move freely since the valves are normally open center. This feature provides pressure compensation, but will not hold loads in place when power is lost.

Pressure-Control Valves.   The maximum pressure level of the working fluid sets the upper limit of force exerted by a linear actuator or torque exerted by a rotary actuator or motor. Thus, control of system pressure permits control of the force or torque output of the hydraulic equipment. Two basic types of pressure-control devices are used in underwater hydraulic circuits: pressure-relief valves and pressure regulators. Pressure-relief valves are normally closed; they open when a certain upstream pressure (relief pressure) is exceeded. Pressure regulators are normally open; they close when a certain downstream pressure (regulated pressure) is reached.

Relief valves are used to limit the maximum pressure in a circuit and as safety valves to prevent overpressuring containers, trapped volumes, and valve packages. Figure 5-9 shows several typical safety relief valves used in underwater applications. A relief valve is designed to function smoothly and continuously up to its rated flow. Normally the relief valve is closed until the pressure level approaches a preset value. At that point the valve begins to open and creates an orifice between the high-pressure supply and a lower-pressure area, usually the return line. As the system pressure increases, the orifice size increases, increasing flow through the valve. When the system pressure drops, the valve closes.

Relief valves may have metal-on-metal valve seats, metal-on-elastomer valve seats (so-called soft seat or zero leakage), or be the spool type. When used for overpressure protection of enclosures such as valve packages, it is important that soft seat valves be used so that they will remain sealed even if the internal, protected pressure is less than the external pressure.

Low-pressure, low-flow relief valves for use as safety valves are readily available in many corrosion-resistant materials that may be used directly in seawater. Higher-pressure, high-flow relief valves used to limit circuit pressure generally have cast iron, bare aluminum, or steel bodies, and are enclosed within the hydraulic power source enclosure or a valve package to protect them from corrosion.

Pressure regulators limit pressure levels in a portion of a circuit by

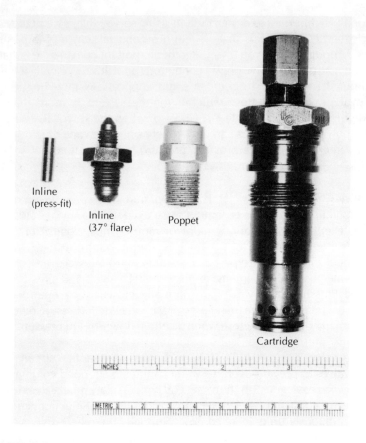

Inline
(press-fit)

Inline
(37° flare)

Poppet

Cartridge

FIGURE 5-9 Typical safety relief valves.

limiting the flow to that circuit. Most pressure regulators and pressure transducers do not have trapped volumes and thus do not require compensating, although this should always be checked. By properly controlling the reference pressure to relief valves and pressure regulators, alternate pressure-control valves, such as counterbalance, sequence, unloading, and flow-directing valves, can be made. Treatment of this subject is left to a hydraulics text.

Flow-Control Valves. When one pump supplies more than one function, there is often a need to provide different amounts of flow to the individual actuators. Flow is controlled by either throttling or diverting. Throttling is used to either restrict the flow into (meter-in) or out of (meter-out) the device whose speed is being controlled. Care must be taken in using meter-out methods in that the return side of the device can be subjected to full or even higher than full system pressure. In bypass control, the fluid is diverted to the reservoir ahead of the device; such a circuit is called a bleed-off circuit.

Throttling flow controls may either be pressure compensated or non-compensated. Noncompensated flow controls, which are simple devices that control flow by restricting or throttling, are the most widely used in underwater circuits. Many commercially available units are so small and lightweight that they are easily incorporated in a standard fitting or a valve manifold (see Figure 5-10). Most behave in a manner similar to that of an orifice. In an orifice, pressure drop increases in proportion to the square of the flow increase. When an orifice is used in a circuit, the flow decreases as the load increases, thereby slowing down the actuator, which is ideal for many remote-control devices. In addition to fixed inline flow-control units, adjustable needle valves are often used for this purpose. Adjustable needle valves can be used as both a shut-off and an adjustable flow control. As the valve is opened, the stem is withdrawn from the seat, providing increased flow area.

Pressure-compensated flow controls are relatively insensitive to circuit pressure. In a typical unit, the pressure drop across a metering orifice is used to shift a pressure-balanced spool against a controlled spring. This spool movement is used to maintain a constant pressure drop across the orifice, which in turn produces a constant flow. For most pressure-compensated flow controls, pressure drop across the orifice, which is determined by spool area, is a relatively small percentage of the system pressure. One caution in using pressure-compensated flow controls in

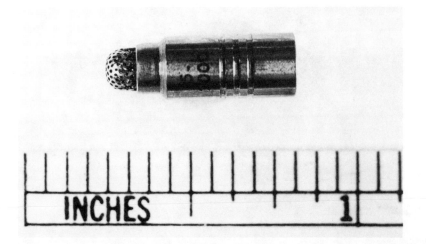

FIGURE 5-10   Small inline flow restrictor.

devices such as manipulators is that when the pressure is directed to the actuator, the speed may start out fast and slow down, which can be highly undesirable. This problem arises because the pressure-compensated flow control moves to the "wide-open" position when there is no flow, and thus in certain types of flow controls there is a brief surge of flow before the spool moves. This is not a problem with noncompensated flow controls.

Pressure-compensated bypass flow regulators control flow by diverting excess pump output to the reservoir. The same basic control orifice and compensator spool are used as in a pressure-compensated flow control, but instead of restricting flow to the actuator, excess flow is diverted to the reservoir. Bypass flow control can only be used in variable-pressure open-center circuits as a meter-in device where it is acceptable to keep the supply pressure only slightly higher than the pressure required to do the work.

Valve Packages. Figures 5-11 and 5-12 show two typical underwater valve packages. The package in Figure 5-11 contains seven three-way valves of a type specially designed for underwater use. The four valves in the left foreground are manifolded into two pairs with lock blocks to form the equivalent of a three-position, four-way valve with a closed center

FIGURE 5-11 Underwater valve package using three-way valves.

FIGURE 5-12 Underwater valve package using four-way valves.

(see Figure 5-8 for the schematic). The small tubing welded into each of the right angle fittings leaving the lock blocks is connected to small relief valves used to ensure that there are no trapped volumes. The valves have all-stainless-steel internal parts as well as unpotted oil-filled coils.

The valve package shown in Figure 5-12 has six industrial-quality, three-position, four-way valves. Contained within the manifold to which the valves are mounted are soft seat lock blocks and noncompensated flow controls. Although the manifold is much more complicated to machine than the valve package shown in Figure 5-11, the valve package in Figure 5-12 is much more compact and lightweight. The industrial valves have carbon steel internal parts and epoxy-potted solenoid coils. The coils were cycled to an ambient pressure of 900 psi (62 MPa) to ensure acceptable life in deep ocean service.

The valve packages each have a cover that seals to the manifold plate and allows the valves to be immersed in nonconductive oil. The oil volume surrounding the valves is connected to a compensator to accommodate expansion and contraction with temperature and depth changes. In addition, the valve package housing is protected by relief valves such that it cannot be overpressured if a hydraulic line leaks, or collapsed if the compensator line is accidentally cut off. It is better to flood the unit with seawater than to collapse it. Experience has shown that the so-called zero inclusion or zero leakage type of hydraulic quick-disconnects makes excellent safety relief valves to prevent collapse. The male portion of the quick-disconnect is mounted to the valve package so that it can be used for filling with compensating oil. When the female half is not connected, the male half can act as a relief valve.

Fluid Conductors

The majority of underwater systems use stainless tubing or flexible hoses for fluid conductors; pipe is seldom used. Because they have proven to be less reliable, hoses are generally used only where relative movement between components is required. The tubing and hoses must be sized to provide a reasonable circuit pressure drop even when operating with oil that has been thickened by the cold temperatures and high ambient pressures at depth (see Figures 3-3, 3-4, and 3-5). Undersize pressure and return lines produce excessive pressure drop and can lead to seal damage on hydraulic motors, which often have the shaft seal cavity connected to the return line. Undersize suction lines can lead to pump cavitation and damage when operated on the surface, but are less of a problem at depth because the high ambient pressures prevent cavitation from occurring. Of course, oversize lines lead to high cost, larger bend radii, and excess weight. The general rule is to size pressure lines for an average flow velocity of 10 to 15 ft/s (3.0 to 4.5 m/s) and suction lines for 2 to 5 ft/s (0.6 to 1.5 m/s).

Rigid Tubing and Tube Fittings.   Hydraulic tubing sizes and materials are standardized. Hydraulic tubing is manufactured in inch-fraction sizes classified by the outside diameter in $^1/_{16}$-inch increments (size " -8" $= ^8/_{16}$ or ½ inch). The thickness of the tubing required can be calculated from the formula $t = (P \times D) \div (2 \times M \times S)$, where D is the outside diameter in inches, M is the safety factor, S is the material tensile strength in psi, P is the system pressure in psi, and t is the thickness in inches. The safety factor is generally four for aircraft, missile, and industrial applications with minimal hydraulic shock; six for average conditions with normal vibration and impulse shock; and eight for severe shock.

Hydraulic tube fittings are of two general types—threaded or permanent. Permanent fittings are usually welded or brazed in place and cannot be disassembled or easily replaced. Permanent fittings are seldom used in underwater equipment. Threaded fittings are attached to the tube by brazing, flare, or flareless arrangements. Figure 5-13 shows cross sections of several fitting types and Figure 5-14 shows the threaded ends. The brazed fittings are not used extensively underwater because of their cost and the incompatibility of braze material with seawater; braze material can result in a corrosion cell between the braze material and the tube or fitting material. Flare and flareless fittings are both used extensively underwater and are readily available in stainless steel.

The flare angle of flareless fittings may be either 37 degrees or 45 degrees. The 45-degree flare is a Society of Automotive Engineers (SAE) standard used primarily in the automotive industry. Forty-five-degree flare fittings are available primarily in the two-piece and inverted flare configurations shown in Figure 5-13. Thirty-seven-degree flare fittings are used primarily in hydraulics, with the three-piece fitting assembly being used almost exclusively. Only the 37-degree flare angle design should be used for stainless steel tubing where the high work-hardening rate can lead to cracking in 45-degree flares.

The three-piece assembly consists of a nut and a sleeve that clamps the tube to the fitting. The actual sealing pressure is transmitted by the sleeve, which produces a much more uniform loading and allows shorter bends than the two-piece designs. Because of their high reliability and reusability, 37-degree flare fittings are the most widely used type of fitting on submersibles and manipulators. However, when the underwater work system is subject to excessive vibration (often during transit on surface ships), it is sometimes necessary to lockwire the fitting nuts to prevent loosening.

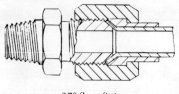

37° flare fitting

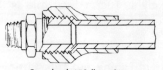

Standard 45° flare fitting

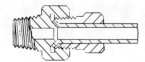

Inverted 45° flare fitting

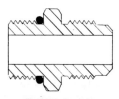

Straight thread
"O"-Ring connector

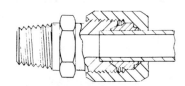

Ferrule compression
fitting

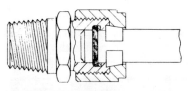

"O"-Ring compression
fitting

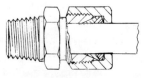

Swagelok ^{R} fitting

FIGURE 5-13 Cross sections of hydraulic fittings.

Flareless fittings, which eliminate the flaring operation, may be the ferrule type or the compression type. In ferrule fittings, sealing is obtained by forcing the edge of the ferrule or sleeve into the tubing well. Most compression types are limited to low pressures, although one manufacturer makes a self-locking type with an O-ring seal. Although flareless fittings are much quicker and easier to use than flares, they have not been as widely used underwater—primarily because an occasional human error leads to an improper seal, causing a catastrophic failure during use. Flare fittings have proven to be less subject to human errors because once the

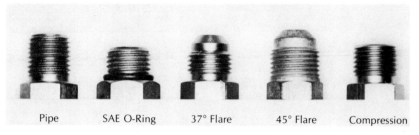

| Pipe | SAE O-Ring | 37° Flare | 45° Flare | Compression |

FIGURE 5-14 Threaded ends of various hydraulic fittings.

flare is properly made and proven leak-tight, it cannot have been assembled improperly.

Tapered pipe threads can be used if care is used in sealing the fitting. The two types of pipe threads in general use are the NPT (American Standard) and NPTF (Dryseal). NPT threads seal by flank contact; NPTF threads seal by a destructive interference fit along the crest. Much care is necessary in preparing threads for pipes to ensure satisfactory service. When the threads are cut on the pipe, burrs are formed and must be removed. When a joint using either type of tapered pipe thread is tightened, an interference fit is obtained. The interference occurs when the mating parts contact each other and interfere to the extent that some force must be used in assembling the joint. Two perfectly machined tapered threads will carry the load over a wide-bearing surface. If the tapers are not equal, a single point of contact results, making the joint difficult to seal. Imperfections in pipe threads account for galling or tearing when the joint is disassembled.

For high-pressure hydraulic applications, a pipe sealer must be used to ensure leak-tight fits. However, improperly applied or excessive pipe sealer or pipe dope can get inside the line and harm pumps and control valves. The authors have used a number of sealers, including epoxy and anaerobic types, and have found a brand called Liquid-O-Ring[R] to be particularly effective in sealing pipe threads. This sealer is a fluorocarbon-based product that includes a lubricant and a corrosion inhibitor.

A straight thread with a lock nut and O-ring gasket can be highly effective in providing a rigid and tight connection between the tube and the component. The military forces have established tube fitting standards as shown in Figures 5-15a and b. These standards have been accepted throughout military and industry, and 37-degree flare fittings are often referred to by the military fitting standard AND10050. The Society of Automotive Engineers (SAE) has adopted a modification to the AND10050 port seal in order to accommodate pipes in closer mechanical locations without a loss of sealing efficiency. The SAE connectors incorporate a narrower skirt on the retaining nut. As a result, an AND-standard fitting can be used in an SAE port, but an SAE fitting cannot be used in an

IST—Internal Straight Threads Gasket Seal MS33650 (AND10050)

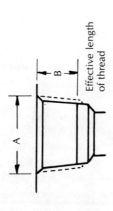

Tube Size	Tube O.D.	Thread MIL-S-7742	A Min. Dia.	B Dia.	C Min.	D Min. Dia.
4	1/4	7/16-20UNF-3B	.828	.562	7/16	.383
6	3/8	9/16-18UNF-3B	.969	.688	15/32	.502
8	1/2	3/4-16UNF-3B	1.188	.875	9/16	.682
10	5/8	7/8-14UNF-3B	1.344	1.000	5/8	.797
12	3/4	1-1/6-12UN-3B	1.625	1.234	11/16	.972
16	1	1-5/16-12UN-3B	1.910	1.487	11/16	1.222
20	1-1/4	1-5/8-12N-3B	2.270	1.800	11/16	1.534
24	1-1/2	1-7/8-12N-3B	2.560	2.050	3/4	1.784
28	1-3/4	2-1/4-12UN-3B	3.010	2.425	13/16	2.159
32	2	2-1/2-12UN-3B	3.480	2.675	15/16	2.409

IPT—Internal Pipe Threads AND10053

Nominal Pipe Size	Threads Per Inch	A Max. Dia.	B
1/8	27	13/32	9/32
1/4	18	9/16	7/16
3/8	18	11/16	7/16
1/2	14	7/8	9/16
3/4	14	1-1/16	37/64
1	11-1/2	1-5/16	23/32
1-1/4	11-1/2	1-43/64	47/64
1-1/2	11-1/2	1-29/32	3/4
2	11-1/2	2-3/8	25/32

IST—Internal Straight Threads
(Gasket Seal)
MS33649

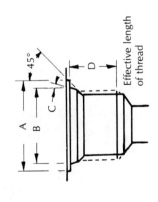

Tube Size	Tube O.D.	Thread MIL-S-8879	A Min. Dia.	B Dia.	C Min.	D Min. Dia.
4	1/4	7/16-20UNJF-3B	.828	.562	37/64	.389
6	3/8	9/16-18UNJF-3B	.969	.688	39/64	.508
8	1/2	3/4-16UNJF-3B	1.188	.875	23/32	.689
10	5/8	7/8-14UNJF-3B	1.344	1.000	13/16	.805
12	3/4	1-1/16-12UNJF-3B	1.625	1.234	7/8	.981
16	1	1-3/8-12UNJ-3B	1.910	1.487	7/8	1.231
20	1-1/4	1-5/8-12UNJ-3B	2.270	1.800	7/8	1.543
24	1-1/2	1-7/8-12UNJ-3B	2.560	2.050	7/8	1.794
32	2	2-1/2-12UNJ-3B	3.480	2.675	29/32	2.419

IST—Internal Straight Threads
(Gasket Seal)
MS16142 SAE

Tube Size	Tube O.D.	Thread	A Min. Dia.	B Min. Dia.	C	D Min.
4	1/4	7/16-20UNF-2B	.664	.563	12°	.454
6	3/8	9/16-18UNF-2B	.809	.688	12°	.500
8	1/2	3/4-16UNF-2B	1.025	.875	15°	.562
10	5/8	7/8-14UNF-2B	1.170	1.000	15°	.656
12	3/4	1-1/16-12UN-2B	1.458	1.250	15°	.750
16	1	1-5/16-12UN-2B	1.746	1.500	15°	.750
20	1-1/4	1-5/8-12UN-2B	2.180	1.875	15°	.750
24	1-1/2	1-7/8-12UN-2B	2.466	2.125	15°	.750
32	2	2-1/2-12UN-2B	3.192	2.750	15°	.750

FIGURE 5-15a Standard porting dimensions.

FLD—Flared Tube Connection
MS33656 (AND10056) SAE 37

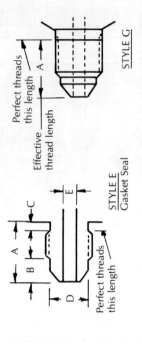

STYLE E
Gasket Seal

Perfect threads this length

Effective thread length

STYLE G

Tube Size	Tube O.D.	THREAD	A	B	C	D Dia.	E Dia.
4	1/4	7/16-20UNF-3A	.550	.193	.075	.359	.172
6	3/8	9/16-18UNF-3A	.556	.198	.083	.476	.297
8	1/2	3/4-16UNF-3A	.657	.253	.094	.654	.391
10	5/8	7/8-14UNF-3A	.758	.266	.107	.767	.484
12	3/4	1-1/16-12UN-3A	.864	.315	.125	.938	.609
16	1	1-5/16-12UN-3A	.911	.315	.125	1.188	.844
20	1-1/4	1-5/8-12UN-3A	.958	.367	.125	1.501	1.078
24	1-1/2	1-7/8-12UN-3A	1.083	.378	.125	1.750	1.312
28	1-3/4	2-1/4-12UN-3A	1.208	.451	.125	2.125	1.547
32	2	2-1/2-12UN-3A	1.333	.461	.125	2.375	1.781

EPT—External Pipe Threads
MS33677 (AND10077)

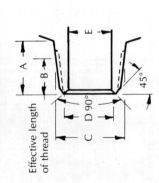

Effective length of thread

Nominal Pipe Size	Threads Per Inch	A	B Ref.	C Min. Dia.	D Min. Dia.	E Dia.
1/8	27	.391	.2639	.405	.240	.188
1/4	18	.594	.4018	.540	.334	.281
3/8	18	.609	.4078	.675	.459	.406
1/2	14	.781	.5337	.840	.615	.531
3/4	14	.797	.5457	1.050	.802	.719
1	11-1/2	.984	.6828	1.315	1.021	.938
1-1/4	11-1/2	1.016	.7068	1.660	1.334	1.250
1-1/2	11-1/2	1.031	.7235	1.900	1.584	1.500
2	11-1/2	1.062	.7565	2.375	2.021	1.938

BST—U.S. Bureau of Standards High Pressure Tube Coupling

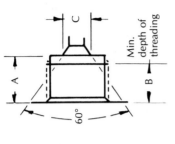

Tube Size	Tube O.D.	Thread	A	B	C
4	1/4	9/16-18	7/16	.344	3/16
6	3/8	3/4-16	9/16	.468	9/32
8	1/2	1-1/8-12	3/4	.625	7/16
9	9/16	1-1/8-12	3/4	.625	7/16
16	1	1-15/16-12	2-13/32	1.125	—

FLS—Flareless Tube Connection MS33514

Tube Size	Tube O.D.	Thread	A	B	C Ref.	D	E	F
4	1/4	7/16-20UNF-3A	.453	.075	.319	.261	.234	.187
6	3/8	9/16-18UNF-3A	.469	.083	.441	.386	.250	.297
8	1/2	3/4-16UNF-3A	.562	.094	.601	.514	.305	.422
10	5/8	7/8-14UNF-3A	.625	.107	.727	.641	.350	.500
12	3/4	1-1/16-12UN-3A	.688	.125	.852	.766	.350	.656
16	1	1-5/16-12UN-3A	.688	.125	1.102	1.016	.415	.875
20	1-1/4	1-5/8-12UN-3A	.688	.125	1.355	1.270	.415	1.093
24	1-1/2	1-7/8-12UN-3A	.688	.125	1.604	1.520	.485	1.344
32	2	2-1/2-12UN-3A	.688	.125	2.108	2.022	.485	1.813

FIGURE 5-15b Standard porting dimensions.

FIGURE 5-16 Straight thread O-Ring porting tool.

AND-standard port. The tool shown in Figure 5-16 facilitates manufacturing the straight thread sealing threads. The advantages of the O-ring ports over pipe threads include: less threading is required than for a pipe-fitting connection; less torque is required to produce a leakproof connect; the O-ring port allows unlimited reassembly without deterioration of the threads; angular outlet fittings can be positioned without impairing sealing; and the sealing effect increases with increased system pressure.

Hose and Hose Fittings.   In addition to permitting relative motion between components, hoses can reduce vibration transmission, ease routing problems, help to absorb hydraulic shocks, and can be used where disconnections are frequently made. A typical hose consists of an innertube for the conducting fluid, a reinforcement for the innertube, and a cover to protect the reinforcement. The innertube must be flexible, able to withstand high and low temperatures, and compatible with the fluid. The reinforcement consists of natural or synthetic fibers or metal wires braided, spiral wound, or wrapped. Two particular types of hoses have proved to

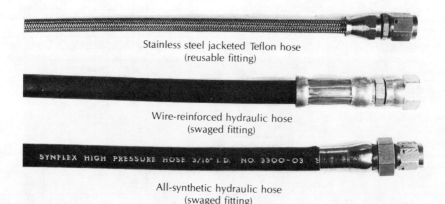

Stainless steel jacketed Teflon hose
(reusable fitting)

Wire-reinforced hydraulic hose
(swaged fitting)

All-synthetic hydraulic hose
(swaged fitting)

FIGURE 5-17   Typical hose and hose fittings.

hold up well in submerged services. One is made entirely of synthetic materials such as Parker Hannifin's Parflex[R] hose or Samuel Moore's Synflex[R] hose; the other is stainless steel jacketed aircraft cable (see Figure 5-17). Unfortunately, both types have their limitations. The all-synthetic hoses are often not as tough and kink more easily than standard hydraulic hose. The stainless jacketed hose does not have an abrasion shield, and tends to accelerate the corrosion of less noble materials it contacts as well as to develop crevice corrosion between wire layers, resulting in catastrophic failure when the hose is not carefully maintained. Even with these limitations, however, both types of hoses have acceptable life in most applications.

Hoses are coupled together by metal components called hose fittings. A hose fitting consists of two major parts: the portion that grips the hose, and the portion that provides the connector for attaching to other fittings. Forces acting to burst the hose are resisted by the reinforcement. The hose fitting must be installed with sufficient grip to prevent blowoff. The two basic families of fittings are (1) permanently attached and (2) reusable (see Figure 5-17). Medium-pressure screwed-together reusable fittings require no special preparation; they are suitable for hydraulics at pressures up to 5000 psi (34 MPa) and temperature ranges from -65 to $+250°F$ (-53 to $+121°C$). High-pressure fittings require gripping onto the hose wire reinforcement for maximum joint strength. To do this, either the fitting bites through the hose cover or the cover is removed in the gripping area. High-pressure nonreusable fittings are usually factory assembled using a special hydraulic press, but portable laboratory-sized units are also available. Readily available fitting materials are generally carbon steel; however, for some hoses, stainless steel fittings are available, generally by special order.

SEALS

O-ring seals are the workhorse of the underwater sealing systems. O-rings are excellent for positive containment under low or high pressure in static sealing applications, and are fairly good, although somewhat limited in life, in dynamic applications. In deep submergence applications, 90-durometer rubber is often used in place of the common industrial grade of 70-durometer rubber to provide a higher contact pressure and to be less subject to taking a permanent set with time. It is important that sufficient squeeze be provided since the O-ring can be expected to decrease in volume about 1 percent per 3000 psi (21 MPa) of hydrostatic pressure change in addition to the volume changes due to temperature changes.

In many cases, flat gaskets are used for sealing underwater equipment, particularly in diaphragm or rolling diaphragm pressure compensators.

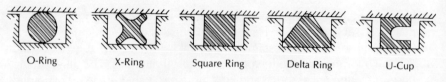

O-Ring   X-Ring   Square Ring   Delta Ring   U-Cup

ELASTOMERIC RING SEALS

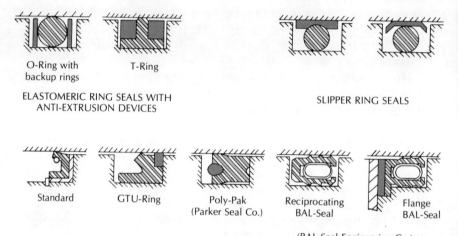

O-Ring with   T-Ring
backup rings

ELASTOMERIC RING SEALS WITH   SLIPPER RING SEALS
ANTI-EXTRUSION DEVICES

Standard   GTU-Ring   Poly-Pak   Reciprocating   Flange
                    (Parker Seal Co.)   BAL-Seal   BAL-Seal

(BAL-Seal Engineering Co.)

LIP SEALS

FIGURE 5-18 Various types of seals. (Adapted from Buchter 1979.)

When using flat gaskets, it is important to have the clamping flanges sufficiently stiff to clamp the gasket uniformly around the sealing edges. In addition, it is prudent to have the flange designed such that it bottoms out metal-to-metal (or plastic-to-plastic in the case of plastic housings) when the gasket has the proper amount of squeeze. This will prevent the gasket from extruding from the joint by over tightening. In many applications a continuous raised bead is provided on the mating surface of one flange to ensure a line squeeze completely around the gasket—a sort of O-ring in reverse.

When it is desired to minimize O-ring wear and friction in dynamic applications, slipper rings can be installed between the O-ring and the mating surface, as shown in Figure 5-18. Slipper rings are designed to be used in standard O-ring grooves, and are very effective where adequate lubrication is unavailable. The authors have found slipper rings to work well in both rotary and linear applications where the mating shaft has a microfinish of RMS 8 or better.

When O-rings are used in high-pressure dynamic environments, a

FIGURE 5-19   Flange-mounted, spring-loaded lip seal. (BAL-Seal Engineering Co.)

backup ring is often used to prevent extrusion into the mating gaps (see Figure 5-18). Backup rings are available as solid rings, split rings, or spiral-turn rings. Both the split and spiral-turn designs eliminate the need of a split assembly for installing the backup ring.

While Buna N is selected for most of the O-ring applications, the slipper seals and backup rings are usually made from a fluorocarbon resin. The almost chemical inertness (see Table 4-2) of Teflon^R TFE fluorocarbon resins has led to its use in seals of all types. The wide temperature range in which these materials can operate and their low coefficient of friction make them ideal for many lip, cup, and ring types of seals.

Lip seals, especially the spring-loaded type, have received a large amount of use in reciprocating and rotary applications underwater. Figure 5-19 shows a flanged-mounted type of lip seal used very successfully by the authors in several rotary applications. This seal has a spring-loaded lip that ensures continued contact with the shaft. This spring loading is necessary for fluorocarbon-based materials, since they tend to take a set and are not as resilient as the elastomers. The spring-loaded type of seal should always be installed with the spring directed toward the sealed volume to prevent damage to the spring by seawater.

Extreme caution must be used when installing lip seals. It is very easy to damage the lip, thereby preventing proper sealing, and the seal will not give or comply to seal off the damaged area as O-rings or gaskets often do. It is necessary to have proper lead-in surfaces on bores and rods or to use special insertion tools to prevent slicing or damaging the seal during assembly; this is especially important when slipping a multi-ringed manifold into a rotary union.

TOOLBITS

Depending upon the work to be done, many types of toolbits may be required to perform an underwater task. In most cases, the toolbits are selected from commercially available equipment with little regard to long-term underwater life. That is, they are considered as throw-away items. Two reasons lead to this method of using toolbits: (1) corrosion-resistant materials often do not have the strength and toughness to withstand the loads or to maintain the edge required; and (2) the development of new toolbit alloys is a long-term, evolutionary, expensive process. In some specific instances, however, this method of using toolbits is beginning to change. An example is the development of a drill-tap-bolt arrangement for attaching a padeye to a sunken object (Figure 5-20). In this case it was recognized that a considerable amount of time could be saved in attaching a lifting padeye if the drilling, tapping, and bolting could all be accomplished in one operation. Thus, a tool was developed that incorpo-

FIGURE 5-20   Drill-tap-bolt padeye.

rated a suction cup evacuated by a seawater pump to hold the padeye in place while a manipulator-operated rotary impact tool is used to drill, tap, and bolt the padeye to the object.

A discussion of a few of the commonly used underwater toolbits along with some of their selection criteria follows.

Brushes

Many types of brushes are commercially available, and each size and kind of brush is designed for a specific action. Most underwater jobs involve cleaning, including removing marine growth, rust, and paint. This type of work requires a harsher brushing action than provided by the majority of commercial brushes. Steel wire is the most commonly used brush material, although various types of organic and synthetic bristles as well as stainless steel are available.

Brushes typically are available in three shapes—wheel, cup, and end. Only the wheel and cup are used extensively underwater. Selection of a wheel or cup depends upon the manipulator and tool configuration. For a manipulator-operated tool with the output shaft parallel to the jaws of the manipulator, it is often easiest to use a cup brush. Cup brushes can work with the axis perpendicular to the surface, and typically are designed for heavy-duty cleaning operations. When a manipulator-operated tool has the output shaft perpendicular to its jaws, a wheel-type brush is often used. As the speed of the brush is increased, the wires become stiffer and the face harder because of the centrifugal force. It also provides faster brushing action. The light gage wire at high speed may give results as good as a coarser wire at low speeds. However, as shown in Figure 2-13, viscous drag increases dramatically with speed underwater. Faster action can be obtained without increasing speed by using heavier wire. Viscous drag can be minimized by using brushes in which the wire is potted in an elastomer. Figure 5-21 shows a stainless steel wheel-type brush and a wheel-type brush that is reinforced by a tough, elastomer material. Both are useful in removing corrosion, scale, and other adhering materials. The elastomer reinforcement is also useful in protecting the bristles as well as in cutting down the friction drag in water.

Grinding Wheels and Discs

The action of a grinding wheel is very similar to that of a milling cutter. The wheel is made up of many small abrasive grains bonded together—each one acting as a small cutting tool, removing elongated metal chips. Grinding has advantages not found in other cutting processes. It is an excellent method of cutting such hard materials as wire rope, high-strength steel, and tool steels. It produces smooth finishes and will continue to cut even if materials are not fed at optimum rates. And, because very little feed

FIGURE 5-21   Typical wire brushes.

pressure is required, grinding can be used on light materials that would spring away or can be used by light-duty manipulators or divers that have limited force capability.

An abrasive is a hard material that can be used to cut or wear away other materials. Aluminum oxide and silicone carbide are the two most common abrasives used in grinding wheels, with aluminum oxide being predominant. Aluminum oxide is slightly softer than silicon carbide, but it is much tougher. There are many different sizes and shapes of grinding wheels, with straight wheels, cup wheels, mounted point wheels, and fiber-reinforced cutoff wheels being the most widely used underwater.

As discussed in Chapter 2, grinding wheels, especially cutoff wheels, are typically operated at less than their recommended speed underwater to cut down on viscous drag. The combination of slower speed and very effective cooling underwater makes cutoff rates slow by commercial standards. However, wheel life is usually good underwater.

Metal Cutting Tools

Cutting tools are made from a variety of materials and used in a wide range of applications. The simplest form of the cutting tool is the single-point tool, such as are used in lathes. Multiple-point cutting tools are two or more single-point tools arranged together as a unit; milling cutters and drill bits are examples.

The life of a metal cutting tool is an important factor since considerable time can be lost when a tool must be replaced. Probably the most common problem underwater is tool breakage by heavy loads due to the inability of the diver, manipulator, or tool-operating device to provide the proper alignment and rigidity. Other factors resulting in premature tool failure include improperly grinding the tool angles, loss of hardness due to excessive speed, breaking the tool edge, and excessive wear or abrasion. Breaking the tool edge usually results from too heavy of a cut at breakthrough. Excessive wear can occur when sediment or sand get into the cutting area. If the tool is operated on the deck, it should be flooded with water to keep it cool and to simulate operating conditions.

Single-point tools have not been widely used underwater. Multiple-point tools, such as drill bits and milling cutters, have been widely used.

Drill Bits.   Drilling holes is an important underwater operation. Large numbers of holes are required for bolting in construction and assembly. In salvage operations, holes are required for inserting toggles or lift points.

Drilling is a complex machining process. It is the combined cutting and extrusion of metal at the point of the center of the drill. Metal under the point is first extruded by a high thrust force caused by the feeding motion. The metal then tends to shear under the action of the tool angle. The cutting action along the lips of the drill is like that of other machining processes. The most important type of drill is the twist drill, as shown in Figure 5-22. There are different classes of drills for different operations. Workpiece material may influence the class of drill used, but it usually determines the

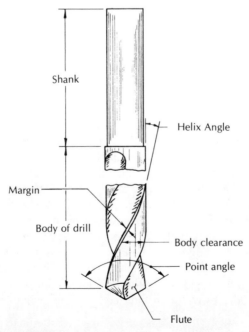

FIGURE 5-22   Drill bit.

point geometry rather than the type of drill. Within the general class of twist drills there are a number of drill types for different operations. The high helix drill has a high helix angle, which improves the cutting efficiency but weakens the drill body; it is used for cutting softer metals. The low helix drill has a lower than normal helix angle and is sometimes used to prevent the tool from running ahead or grabbing when drilling materials such as brass. Heavy-duty drills, which are made by increasing the web thickness, are stronger for severe drilling. Smaller helix angles and thicker webs are used to improve the rigidity. Most drills used today are made of high-speed steel. Carbide tips have been used on drills with success in masonry, nonmetallics, and light alloys. The lack of rigidity and the low cutting speed at the center have not allowed carbides to be widely used for drilling steels.

The general-purpose twist drill has a point angle of 118 degrees, a helix angle of 30 degrees, a lip relief of 12 degrees, and a chisel-edge angle of 135 degrees. Modifications are desirable according to the properties of the work piece. In general, harder materials require a higher point angle, which gives a stronger cutting edge. For example, steel that is quite hard can be drilled to the point angle of 150 degrees. Another property of the helix angle is its effect on chip disposal. Chips can slide more easily up a higher helix drill, and drills of this type are better for drilling deep holes than are tools with a lower helix angle.

There is usually an optimum feed rate for drilling. However, underwater drilling equipment has not been built for a constant feed rate and is usually either hand-held by a diver or held by a manipulator with some given force or pressure. When constant pressure is used to feed the drill, the thrust force must be adjusted to provide the desired feed rate. Typical desirable thrust forces were shown in Figure 2-18 in Chapter 2. As the drill wears, the thrust force that is required to maintain a given feed rises. If the thrust remains constant, the feed rate decreases. A difficulty that occurs when constant pressure feed is used without retarding devices is the sudden increase of tool travel when the drill point breaks through the bottom of the work piece. Since the cutting lips are still in the work piece, the torque increases rapidly and the drill may break or the drill motor may stall. In addition, the metal remaining ahead of the drill may be deformed under the action of the large thrust force, leaving a large burr around the hole.

Underwater drilling provides sufficient cooling that drill bits are seldom damaged by overheating even when the feed pressure is not sufficient to provide a reasonable feed rate. Suction bases, such as the one shown in Figure 1-2, help to provide an optimum feed rate but, to date, no underwater drilling devices with constant feed rate are available.

Milling Cutters.   Milling is a process for removing material with a rotary cutter. Flat or curved surfaces may be produced by milling. Milling

FIGURE 5-23   End mill and hole saw.

can also be used effectively for rapid removal of material or for accurate finishing of smooth surfaces. In milling, each tooth on the cutter removes a small amount of metal with each revolution of the spindle. Two characteristics of milling are the relatively small size of each chip and the interruptions of cutting as the teeth enter and leave the work piece. There is a variation in chip thickness during the cut.

There are many different classes of milling cutters; however, only two—the standard end mill and the circular saw (hole saw)—have been used to a significant extent underwater. The plain milling cutter is a general-purpose cutter for periphery milling operations. The narrow cutters have straight teeth, while the wider cutters have helical teeth. The end mill shown in Figure 5-23 and the spindle-mounted end mill shown in Figure 5-24 have peripherial and end cutting edges. The milling machine must be designed to withstand the large forces involved in cutting without excessive chatter or uneven feeds, and to supply sufficient rotary power at the proper speeds and feeds. It must also be rigid enough to withstand the impacts due to the periodic force variations. Milling can be accomplished by conventional or "up" milling, where the work pieces are fed into the cutter teeth, or by climb or "down" milling, where the work pieces and cutter feed in the

FIGURE 5-24 Underwater milling spindle.

same direction. In up milling, the tooth must start cutting at zero thickness, and actually skids along the surface until sufficient force is built up to allow it to dig in; this roughens the surface. In down milling, the chip is thick at the start so that the tooth end easily penetrates. The cutting force has a larger component along the direction of feed in down milling, requiring a more rigid setup. The chief advantage of up milling is the lower impact encountered as the tooth starts because the chip is thinner initially. The chief reason for underwater milling is to provide a fairly low power input and a controllable method of cutting large holes in bulkheads. The major problem encountered in underwater milling is attaching the milling machine to the sunken object. This problem was overcome on the milling cutter shown in Figure 2-21 through the use of suction cups to penetrate single-point tool bits into the surface to be machined; the tool bits prevented sliding of the machine.

A machining process that is directly comparable to milling is circular sawing. Actually, circular sawing is a milling process in which the axial cut dimension is quite small. A circular sawing bit (hole saw) was shown in Figure 5-23. Circular sawing bits normally operate at slow cutting speeds ranging from 18 ft/min (.09 m/s) for hard material to 134 ft/min (.67 m/s) for softer material.

Taps.   Screw sizes are expressed by the outside diameter and the number of threads per inch. Screw threads are used in fasteners such as bolts and screws. Threads are easy to design and produce. They usually have a V-shape that can make a crevice for corrosion, and therefore are not suited for long-term use without sealers or inhibitors in materials prone to crevice corrosion, such as austenitic stainless steel.

Taps are used to produce internal threads in drilled holes. They may be rotated by hand or by power tools. The tap itself is a hardened piece of carbon or alloy steel resembling a bolt with flutes along the side to provide cutting edges. A taper tap should be used for starting the thread to help ensure straighter starting and more gradual cutting on the threads. For closed bottom or blind holes where it is necessary to have the threads go to the bottom, a bottoming tap should be used. Before a hole can be tapped, it must be drilled with a tap-size drill to remove the excess material from the hole. After the hole is drilled, the tap must be inserted, threaded, and removed, and then the proper bolt or fastener installed. These operations are time consuming and require an extremely accurate positioning capability. Because taps tend to be hard and brittle, there is often excessive breakage in underwater applications. To improve this situation, a device that drills, taps, and fastens in one step was designed for underwater use (see Figure 5-20). This device is typically mounted in a holder, as discussed in the introduction of this chapter, and inserted using a rotary impact wrench. Rotary impact wrenches have proven to be highly effective in driving taps in underwater applications, even though excessive breakage would otherwise be expected.

WRENCHES

Where strength and light weight are required, wrenches are usually made of alloy steels. Wrenches are commonly forged from bar stock, then annealed for machinability and structure prior to machining. They are usually heat-treated to develop hardness, strength, and wear-resistance with toughness. Wrenches require steel with good surface and internal uniformity for reliable service. The most commonly used steels in wrenches are nickel, chrome, chrome molybdenum, chrome vanadium, and nickel chrome molybdenum steels. These steels are usually oil-hardening grades. Because they do not have good inherent corrosion resistance, they must have additional corrosion protection for use in seawater. For protection, they may be cleaned and coated with an anticorrosion material or may be stripped and hard-chrome plated. In either case, they should be rinsed with fresh water after each use and coated with light oil until the next use.

UNDERWATER
WORK SYSTEMS
OF THE FUTURE

THE primary driving forces behind the development of underwater tools and work systems will continue to be resource exploitation, as the continued expansion of the offshore oil industry into deeper waters drives the development of sophisticated remote-control well-head completion and repair systems, and the expansion of military and scientific capabilities in oceans, as the need in military, scientific, and mining applications for more information about the ocean depths drives the development of sophisticated deep ocean work and survey systems. One trend that will lead to improved underwater diving and vehicle tools is that toward the in-situ processing of resources. In the past, offshore resources usually have been brought back to shore for processing; today, tapping and processing or refining of resources on site prior to transport back to shore is being attempted in many areas. Examples of this in-situ processing include the Ocean Thermal Energy Conversion (OTEC) program, which is designed to tap the massive thermal energy storage capacity of the ocean to produce electricity on site, and the manganese nodule recovery systems currently being developed, which will clean and crush the nodules on the ocean floor prior to their transport to a waiting ship or ocean-going processing plant.

It is anticipated that future work will include the emplacement of very large objects on the ocean floor. These objects may include foundations for mineral and energy storage and processing plants, large aquiculture facilities, and large waste processing or dilution facilities. In addition to such large construction, programs are underway to develop systems that will recover larger and larger objects, such as downed aircraft, more economically from deep ocean depths. These programs are expected to lead to the capability of recovering objects weighing as much as 10 tons (9000 kg) from 20,000 ft (6100 m) of seawater.

DIVER TOOLS

Many existing hand-held diver work tools are fairly well developed, and as shown in the earlier chapters, a wide range of tools are commercially available. Although improvements in corrosion resistance, seals, and weight can be made to existing tools, most of the future development of the existing tool types will involve the larger special-purpose tools, such as the drill press shown in Figure 2-2 and the milling machines shown in Figure 2-21. However, new types of tools, especially for nondestructive testing and repair of offshore platforms, are being developed, including ultrasonic thickness- and flaw-detection equipment, which is already in use, and ultrasonic liquid level and identification equipment for application to submerged vessels, which is being developed. In addition, ultrasonic techniques for removing marine growth and for forming images under limited visibility conditions are being investigated. Underwater plasma arc, high-pressure water jet, and laser cutting techniques also offer promise for future cutting tools.

SUBMERSIBLES

At depths beyond about 200 ft (60 m), the safe support of divers is costly. The use of manned submersibles is also costly, especially at depths below about 1000 ft (300 m). Unmanned remotely controlled vehicles have been developed to provide a cost-effective alternative to both divers and manned submersibles for many operations. Such vehicles are becoming highly sophisticated and will continue to be improved in depth capability and reliability. Because a limiting factor for remotely controlled vehicles is the ability of the operator to view operations clearly and to manipulate tools accurately and rapidly, a considerable effort will continue to be directed toward developing improved television systems, improved signal transmission systems including fiberoptics, and improved manipulators. Ultrasonic image-forming techniques for use in turbid water would be especially useful for submersibles. The widespread use of microprocessors also is simplifying many control problems, allowing simplification of the electronics and improvement of vehicle and manipulator control through the use of preprogrammed routines.

Figure 6-1 shows the U.S. Navy's Remote Unmanned Work System (RUWS) vehicle recovering a transponder in 3,000 ft (900 m) of water. This vehicle utilized a simple position-control manipulator and a rate-control grabber (holding the transponder) and, prior to its loss in 15,000 ft (4500 m) of water in 1980, was considered state of the art for the 1970s for vehicles with a 20,000-ft (6100-m) working depth. Larger vehicles with an expanded work capability for deep operations are currently under development, as are experimental unmanned, untethered preprogrammed vehicles. In addition, several bottom crawler vehicles are in use or under consideration and more are anticipated. Bottom crawling provides a stable location capability with increased thrust and position-keeping capability over thruster-controlled vehicles. In addition, bottom crawlers can achieve a significant savings in the power required to maneuver vehicles. The trend

FIGURE 6-1   U.S. Navy's Remote-Controlled Unmanned Work System removing a transponder. (Courtesy of Naval Ocean Systems Center, Hawaii Laboratory.)

in bottom crawlers appears to be away from conventional tracked vehicles to Archimedes screw-propelled units, such as Ocean Mineral Company's deep ocean miner (Sea Technology 1980). Submersible, tool, and manipulator development efforts are expected to be directed toward more compact, lighter units. Microprocessor control of such repetitive motions as tool interchange operations will become common even on simple rate-controlled manipulators.

POWER SOURCES

Power tools and submersibles require power sources. Thus, the development of lightweight, compact energy storage systems and power production equipment will continue to pace the successful development and operation of more compact tool systems and submersibles. The major power sources for underwater equipment will continue to be secondary batteries, fuel cells, nuclear power plants, and shipboard engine generator sets. Batteries and fuel cells are expected to remain the primary energy sources for relatively small untethered deep ocean submersibles, while shipboard generator sets are expected to remain the main power source for tethered submersibles.

MATERIALS

Fiber-reinforced plastics will displace the more conventional metals in many underwater tools, especially for deep applications. The light weight, high strength, corrosion resistance, and improved fabrication techniques of modern reinforced plastics are causing this trend. Similarly, the development of ceramics that are stronger, less brittle, and easier to fabricate could provide the basis for cost-effective seawater-hydraulic systems for diver-held tools.

REFERENCES

BATORI, G. J. (1974). Actuation with a Bang. *Machine Design* 46(31): 49–53.

BLACK, S. A. (1976). *Preliminary Analysis of Seawater Hydraulic Tool Motors.* TM No. 43-77-06, Civil Engineering Laboratory, Naval Construction Battalion Center.

BUCHTER, H. H. (1979). *Industrial Sealing Technology.* New York: Wiley and Sons.

BURLESON, C. W. (1977). *The Jennifer Project.* Englewood Cliffs, N.J.: Prentice-Hall.

BUSBY, R. F. (1976). *Review of Manned Submersible Design, Operations, Safety, and Instrumentation.* Office of the Oceanographer of the Navy, U.S. Coast Guard Underwater Safety Project Report No. OCEANAV 041–6.

CAUDY, D. W.; DESAW, F. A.; MISHLER, H. W.; and RANDALL, M. D. (1969). *Determination of the Feasibility of Shielded-Metal-Arc-Welding and Oxygen-Air Cutting at a Depth of 600 Feet.* Final Report to U.S. Navy under Contract No. N00014-66-C-0199.

CAUDY, D. W., and HACKMAN, D. J. (1976). *A Comparison of the General Electric Underwater Manipulator with the Program and Remote System Underwater Manipulator Used on Work Systems Package.* Unpublished U.S. Navy Report.

CAUDY, D. W., and HACKMAN, D. J. (1977). *Final Design Evaluation, Work Systems Package.* Final Report to U.S. Navy on Contract No. N00953-77-C-0089.

CAUDY, D.W.; CHRISTENSON, B.C.; BALOUGH, S.; EVANS, R.M.; TIERNEY, J.M.; and GLAUBITZ, E.W. (1979). *Underwater Firecracker Welding for Attaching Pipe-Connection Flanges.* Offshore Technology Conference, Paper No. OTC 3468, May 1979.

CEL. (1976). *Tools and Equipment for Underwater Construction and Salvage.* Civil Engineering Laboratory, Naval Construction Battalion Center.

CEL. (1978). *Materials Study for High-Pressure Seawater Hydraulic Tool Motors.* CR 78.012, Civil Engineering Laboratory, Naval Construction Battalion Center.

CEL. (1980). *Development of a Seawater Hydraulic Valve Motor for Diver Tools.* CR 80.015, Civil Engineering Laboratory, Naval Construction Battalion Center.

COOKE, M. A. (1958). *The Science of High Explosives.* American Chemical Society Monograph Series, No. 139. New York: Reinhold.

DALZIEL, C. F. (1962). Transistorized-Residual-Current Trip Device for Low-Voltage Circuit Breakers. In *Transactions of the AIEE* 81: 978–983.

DREYFUSS, HENRY (1960). *The Measure of Man.* New York: Whitney Publications.

EMERSON, H.; ANGEL, T.; and COX, L. (1967). Saturation Diving—A Tool for Underwater Welding and Cutting. In *Proceedings of the Symposium on Underwater Welding, Cutting and Hand Tools,* held at Battelle Memorial Institute, Columbus, Ohio, October 1967.

GOODFELLOW, R. (1977). *Underwater Engineering.* Tulsa: Petroleum Publishing Co.

GRUBBS, C. E. (1977). Wet Welding's Role in Underwater Repair. *Ocean Resources Engineering,* April 1977.

HACKMAN, D. J., and GLASGOW, J. S. (1967). *Tools for Deep Diving Operation.* ASME Paper 67-WA/UNT-8, pp. 1–2.

HACKMAN, D. J. (1969). Power Tools for Divers. *Battelle Research Outlook* 1 (1).

HACKMAN, D. J. (1970). Power Tools Underwater. *Oceanology International* 5(4): 19–21.

HACKMAN, D. J; ESTABROOK, N.; WHEELER, H.; and UHLER, D. (1975). Development of Deep-Ocean Work System. In *Proceedings of the IEEE 1975 Ocean Engineer Conference,* IEEE Ocean '75-573.

HACKMAN D. J.; ADKINS, D. E.; and COLLINS, K. (1977). *Work Tools for Underwater Vehicles.* Paper No. OTC 3036, 9th Annual Offshore Technology Conference, May 1977.

KEMP, W. N. (1945). Underwater Arc Welding. In *Transactions of the Institute of Welding.* 8(4): 152–156.

KENNY, J. E. (1972) *Business of Diving.* Houston: Gulf Publishing, p. 142.

LIFFICK, G. L.; MITTLEMAN, J.; and QUIRK, J. (1974). Diver Tools. In *The Working Diver—1974 Symposium Proceedings,* Marine Technology Society.

MASUBUCHI, K. (1971). Materials to Fight Marine Environments. *Materials Engineering* 73(1): 27–38.

MASUBUCHI, K., and TSAI, C.T. (1977). Interpretive Report on Underwater Welding. *Welding Research Council Bulletin,* No. 224: 1–37.

McQUAID, R. W., and BROWN, C. L. (1972). *Handbook of Fluids and Lubricants for Deep Ocean Applications.* Naval Ship Research and Development Center.

MEHNEIT, T.H. (1972). *Handbook of Fluid-Filled, Depth/Pressure-Compensating Systems for Deep Applications.* Naval Ship Research and Development Center.

MEISEL, W. H. (1972). Hydraulic Actuators. *Machine Design* 44(22): 41–44.

MISHLER, H. H., and RANDALL, M. D. (1969). Underwater Joining and Cutting. *Battelle Research Outlook* 1(1).

MITTLEMAN, J. (1978). Field Use of the NAVSEA Diver Tool Package. In *The Working Diver—1978 Symposium Proceedings.* Marine Technology Society.

MYERS, J. J. HOLM, C. H.; and McALLISTER, R. F., eds. (1969). *Handbook of Ocean and Underwater Engineering.* New York: McGraw-Hill.

NAVSEA (1971). *SALVOPS 71.* Naval Sea Systems Command Report No. 0994-012-6030.

NAVSHIPS (1969). *Underwater Cutting and Welding. U.S. Navy.* Naval Ship System Command Report No. Q929-000-8010.

NAVSHIPS (1979). *Recovery of Deep Research Vehicle Alvin.* Naval Ship System Command Report No. 0994-004-5010.

PENZIAS, W., and GOODMAN, M. W. (1973). *Man Beneath the Sea.* New York: Wiley Interscience.

RODMAN, M. F. (1944). Underwater Cutting of Metals. *Journal of the American Welding Society* 7: 603–669.

ROZNER, A. G., and HELMS, H. H. (1976). *Pyronol Torch—A Non-Explosive Underwater Cutting Tool.* Paper No. OTC-2705, Offshore Technology Conference.

SCHUMACKER, B. W. (1967). Electron Beams as Tools for Underwater Cutting and Welding-Laboratory Tests. In *Proceedings of the Symposium on Underwater Welding, Cutting and Hand Tools,* held at Battelle Memorial Institute, Columbus, Ohio, October 1967.

Sea Technology 21(9), p. 9 (September 1980).

SMITH, H. D. (1968). Useful Underwater Work and CURV. *Journal of Ocean Technology* 2(4): 19–23.

TUTHILL, A. H., and SCHILLMOLLER, C. M. (1965). *Guidelines for Selection of Marine Materials.* Paper presented at the Ocean Sciences and Ocean Engineering Conference, Marine Technology Society, Washington, D.C.

UHLER, D. G. (1976). The Work Systems Package. In *The Working Diver—1976 Symposium Proceedings.* Marine Technology Society.

UHLER, D. G. (1978). Underwater Ship Husbandry. In *The Working Diver—1978 Symposium Proceedings*. Marine Technology Society.

UHRICH, R. W. (1977). *Manipulator Development at the Naval Undersea Center*. Naval Undersea Technical Paper No. TP553.

U. S. ARMY MATERIAL COMMAND. (1963). *Propellant-Actuated Devices*. AMCP 706-270.

WERNLI, R. L. (1978). NOSC Informal Progress Report, Fiscal Year 1977; Work Systems Package (WSP) Program, Naval Ocean Systems Center TN360.

WERNLI, R. L.; BERTSCHE, W. R.; LOGAN, K. P.; and PESCH, A. J. (1978). *Evaluation of the Design and Undersea Work Capability of the Work Systems Package*. Naval Ocean Systems Center Technical Report 214.

WERNLI, R. L. (1979). *Development of a Design Baseline for Remotely Controlled Underwater Work Systems*. Paper presented at IEEE/MTS Oceans '78 Conference.

WERNLI, R. L. (1980). Designing for Remote Work in the Deep Ocean. *Mechanical Engineering* 102(2): 27–34.

WILLOUGHBY, R. A. (1972). Air Motors. *Machine Design* 44(2): 218–220.

WILSON, F. W., and HARVEY, P. D., eds. (1959). *Tool Engineers Handbook*. New York: McGraw-Hill.

WINGET, C. L.; BERTSCHE, W. R.; LOGAN, K. P.; and PESCH, A. J. (1977). *Operator Performance in Undersea Manipulator Systems: Studies of Control Performance with Visual Feedback*. Woods Hole Oceanographic Institute Report No. WHOI-77-6.

WODTKE, C. H. (1960). Constricted Arc Process Cuts Metals Underwater. *Metal Progress* 78(6): 91–93.

INDEX